STRE~~~~~~
FROM WITHIN

By Ruby McKenzie

'One million people commit suicide every year'
The World Health Organization

Ruby McKenzie

Published by
Chipmunkapublishing
PO Box 6872
Brentwood
Essex CM13 1ZT
United Kingdom

http://www.chipmunkapublishing.com

Edited by Jurita Bennett

STRENGTH FROM WITHIN

THE ABUSE

_____

I have started to write this book about six times now over the past ten years and I know the reason behind it you see I had so much more to deal with in my life as I could not even imagine what more I had to cope with .

Also I wish to dedicate this book to all who have helped me regarding the issues which I am about to write about also I sincerely hope that any one who is reading this and finding themselves in any of the situations that this book is about that they find faith and the courage to deal with it just as I did so may god and his angels be with you at this time in your life and through out your life time .

The day that I was born should have been the most joyous day for my parents but now I realize that my mother had come to rue the day I was born as she had made this very clear to me over the years how she came to hate me and how she could not stand the thought of me being near her as she always pushed me away from her since I was a small child as far as I was concerned my own mother rejected me from day one.

My name is Abigail I am the second oldest of six children I was brought up with my four brothers and one sister from an early age I felt I did not belong within the family I did not know where I belonged but it certainly was not within this family.

As far back as I can remember I was just four years old when my mother told me that she hated me and that she should of drowned me at birth and then she would hit me real hard across the face I never knew what I had done wrong for my own mother to just turn on me like this.

By the time I started school I was a very nervous child and an unhappy one what with the beating from my mother and the rejection I was so shy and I was so afraid of making a mistake more often or not I had home work to do but that was a waste of time as my mother or father never ever showed me where I was going wrong in my school work they were just not interested as for my mother she just kept telling me I was thick and worthless that I would never come to anything in my older years .

One day after I had washed the dishes my mother came into the kitchen to check on my progress and to check that I had washed the dishes right she picked up a plate from the draining board and she threw it back into the water and she told me there was still food on it and to do it again then she hit me across the face then she started to shout that I was useless and hopeless and it was all my fault I had no idea what she was going on about when she said it was all my fault then she told me to go straight to bed after I washed the

STRENGTH FROM WITHIN

dishes.

That was my life for years physical abuse and mental abuse from my mother nothing changed the only different thing was as I got older and the beating got worse much worse.

As for my father he would play games with me and he would throw me up into the air

also from a very early age how he used to throw me onto the couch and tell me to lie still so that he can touch me he would lie beside me on the couch and touch me down below he told me it was a game and not to tell any one about it and I never did I Must have been about five years old when he started his games with me and this went on for years before I realized what he was doing was wrong and this was why my mother meant by saying it was all my fault .

The physical and sexual abuse lasted for years I could not take any more so I had decided to runaway I went to see my aunt Helen she was my mothers aunt she was always good to me she would give me things and let me stay over at the weekends when I was younger I went to aunt Helens and told her I hated my mother and told her my mother was always hitting me for no reason but I never told her about my father as I was so afraid she would hate me and blame me too I could not bear the rejection from my favourite aunt so I kept my mouth close regarding the sexual abuse from my father.

My aunt gave me my tea and she told me I must go home as my mother was not that bad and then she told me I must of done something wrong for my mother to hit me this advice did not help me in any way in fact it made me feel worse it made me feel as if it was my own fault that I was getting the beatings so I decided on my way home that I must be as bad as my mother was saying I did not go home I just wandered round and round as I had no intentions of going home I did not like my parents and worst of all I did not like me in fact I did not know who me was I was lost I had no where to go I walked and walked until came to a park and it had one long hedge in it as it was getting dark I lay down under the hedge and curled myself into a ball to keep myself warm I lay there thinking about my life I did not have a life I just existed and far as I was concerned this existence was just pure hell I eventually fell asleep and when I woke up it was pitch black and it was so cold I got up from under the hedge and I wandered out of the park into the street as I was glad of the light I had been walking for about twenty minutes when all of a sudden this police car drove right up next to me then this police woman got out and asked me why I was walking about at that time of the morning I did not answer her she told me to get into the back of the police car I was glad to do it just to get some warmth into my body as I was so cold once inside the car the police woman asked me my name again I could not tell her as I knew she would take me home that's when she threatened me with the police cells if I did not tell her I had no option but to tell her as the thought of the police cells frightened me more than going home even though going home I knew what was in store for me I did tell the police woman that my mother and father were always hitting me she told me to be quiet and to give them my address.

We arrived at my home sometime in the early morning they took me to the front door I was absolutely petrified by this time and I was shaking when the police knocked on my parent door my father opened the door he looked very very angry I could not look him in the eye I just hung my head and as I walked into the hall my father told the police to go into the living room and he told me to go into the kitchen as I was going into the kitchen the living room door closed I tried to make out what my parent and the police were saying but I could not hear anything but mumbled voices I was sitting in the kitchen for about twenty minutes when I heard the living room door opening and the front door closing I started to cry at this point as I knew what was coming my mother walked into the kitchen and she walloped me real hard in the back and she told me that I was a waste of space and to get down and scrub the kitchen floor this was about four in the morning after I scrubbed the floor I went to bed it was as if I just got into to bed when my mother told me to get up with the rest of the family and get breakfast it was while I was washing dishes my mother told me I was not going to school as my father wanted to see me and after I had finished the dishes I had to go up to my room and wait on my father I tried to make doing the dishes last long as possible as I did not want to face my father eventually I did finish washing the dishes and then I went upstairs to my room I just sat on my bed when I heard my father come up the stairs and into my room we just looked at each another then I watched as my father took off his belt he then told me to lie across this chair in my room I knew I had to do as he said as it would be the worst for me he then started to hit me with it he was hitting me across my back and my body I felt the pain in my elbow as the belt connected with my elbow bone I was screaming as this point and I just prayed for some one to come and help me but no one came no one heard my prayer my mother came into the room and that's when the beatings stopped .

My father walked out of the room I was sobbing breaking my heart but no one cared all my mother said was clean the rooms out then go to bed there was no feelings in her voice nothing then she turned and walked out of the room I could hardly lift the brush to sweep the carpet because of the pain in my arm and my body but I knew I had to do it as my mother would be up to check on my cleaning as I went to bed I could not lie down I

STRENGTH FROM WITHIN

was totally in pain but I was glad of the solitude .

I must of fell asleep due to the fact I was crying a long time I was not long awake when my brothers came home from school and my big brother asked me what had happened and why I ran away I told him that I hated my parents and he just shrugged his shoulders my brothers and sister never did show any interest in me it was as long as I was taking the beating from my parents then my parents were leaving them alone they did not care about me in fact who did care about me .

One Saturday night my parents were out and as usual my big brother David and I were left to look after the other kids and one of my friends Rose came to stay the night as my parents were out drinking with her parents.

My friend rose and I went to bed and we eventually fell asleep when I was awoken by a noise it was dark and I wondered what was happening when I heard my friend Rose crying when I eventually got used to the dark I saw the outline of my father and I smelt the fumes of the drink from his breath my friend told me that my father was touching her under the covers I told my father to go away as Rose was frightened he got up from the floor and he left the room after he left the room I pleaded with Rose not to say any thing as I was frightened I would get the blame for what my father was trying to do to her that night I was afraid to go to sleep all that night as I was so afraid that he would come back into the room I was so tired the next morning I could hardly keep my eyes open due to the lack of sleep after I gave every one there breakfast my friend Rose told me she was going home I was so afraid she would tell some one what my father done to her I was on heckle pins all that day but as the day turned to night I realized that she must of kept quiet about the whole episode I never did find out if she said anything but she never mentioned it to me again and she never stayed the night again.

A few days later I was sitting in the living room when my mother told me to go and make her a cup of tea I got up and after I made the tea and I took it back into the living room and lay it down on the fender of the fire place as I walked back into the kitchen to tidy up when I heard a sound behind me it was my mother she asked me what is this muck meaning the tea and then she threw the cup at me and it bounced of my sore elbow and I started to cry she told me to shut up and then she slapped me across the face and told me to make her another cup of tea then she walked out of the room I was left standing there with the tea dripping off me and as I tried to lift the kettle I could hardly lift it because of the pain in my elbow.

One day the carnival came to town and my mother said she would take us to the carnival and that we had to behave all that week I tried my best to please her as I knew she would not let me go if I angered her in any way

I tried my best to keep her happy sure I did on the day of the outing I was in the bathroom washing my hair when my mother told me to get out as she wanted to use the toilet as there was shampoo in my hair I could not see a thing and I tried to get out of her way as I never moved quick enough she got hold of my hair and threw me across the bathroom I told her to leave me alone but this just made her worse she screamed at me she hated me and wished I was dead and then she had her hands around my throat and she was trying to strangle me I thought she was going to kill me and at that point I really wished that she would as I just wanted out of this life I wanted away from the pain that I was carrying inside of me she stopped then she kicked me and told me to get out I ran from the bathroom like a scared rabbit.

As I lay on my bed and I wished I was dead as I was all sore from the beating how much more could I take how much more did I have to suffer so before I fell asleep I prayed to god that may I never wake up again that's how I felt I was sad and I was alone even though I had my brothers and sister I was still alone I did not communicate much with my brothers and sister as far as I was concerned they were not part of my life they did not have to live the hell I had to go through and as far as I was concerned they never cared about me or what I was suffering and if they did they never showed it in any way.

A few hours later my mother shouted on me to go to the shops as I got up to go I was all sore with every step I took I was in agony but still I had to make out I was fine and not in pain because if my mother saw me crying she would hit me again I went to the shops and when I got back my brothers told me they were going to the carnival and that I was not going as I had been bad and they were smirking at me as they said it I just looked at them and I walked out to the back yard to get the washing off the rope and when I came back my mother told me I was to watch my younger sister Joan as she was just about two at the time .

The time had come for my mother and brothers to leave for the carnival and I was told to listen out for my sister as she was sleeping my mother was out of the house about twenty minutes when my father told me to come over to him I told him to leave me alone he just ignored this remark as I just stood there he told me to get over to him

I did as he told me he then told me to go into his and my mothers room and that I had to go and lie on the bed and wait on him as he wanted to show me something I did as he told me and he came into the room and he put his hand up my skirt and he pulled my pants to the side and he took out his penis and he held it in his hand and he told me that he was going to put it inside of me and that it will not hurt for long as he put it into me I was crying I told him it was sore he told me just to be quiet I wanted to tell him to leave me alone I was screaming inside I hated my father for what he was doing to me I was praying for my sister to wake up cry do something but there was no sound just my father having sex with me after he had finished he just rolled of me got up and walked out of the room then he told me to go and wash myself I did as I was told and I got my sister up as I did not know what else to do I needed her up so that I can forget what had just happened I needed some sort of normality in my life at that moment I was so mixed up inside .

My mother and brothers came in and they were all excited about the outing I told them to shut up as I was not interested in there outing when in all honestly I was hurting deep inside but I could no tell any one as it was my own fault.

The next day my mother told me to come into the living room when my brothers went out to play I went to see her and she was sitting on her chair beside the fire and she told me to come across to her I was very hesitant to do this as I knew what she was like she told me to move quickly or else it would be worst for me if I did not do as she asked as I moved across to her she slapped me across the face telling me I was a slut and that I was no better than my father I was crying she told me to get the kitchen floor scrubbed and to shut up and then she told me it was my fault my father was touching me no one else's I just stood with my head bowed I was so ashamed I felt dirty and worthless and I thought no one will ever like me how I hated myself she blamed me and I took the blame .

The abuse lasted for years and years I Must have been about fourteen when I decided to runaway again as I had taken more than enough of the abuse I went back to see my aunt Helen and I told her how my mother was always hitting me and that it was worse than ever I told her how my mother would always tell me that she hated me aunt Helen told me that she would not mean what she said regarding hating me as she had her hands full with my brothers and sister and that I needed to talk to my mother I told her that was a waste of time and just told her I was not going home I did not have a home as far as I was concerned it was not my home I didn't know where home was and it certainly was not there .

So once again I found myself under the same hedge in the park as I would rather sleep under that hedge than go back to my parents house I lay down on the ground and I started to think about what was going on at home I just could not think as my mind was going round and round I tried to look for some kind of reason and answers to what my life was all about but no answers came to me just this continue buzzing in my head and my head hurt some how I managed to sleep but not for long as the rain woke me up I was getting wet and I had to get out of the rain and find some sort of shelter as it was cold dark and like me miserable outside as well as inside I went in searching for a place to keep dry and where that place was I did not know I had to stay away from the road as I could not afford to be picked up from the police again as I did not want to be taken back home again I found a shelter in which I was able to sit in and while I was there I heard a noise like a radio and people talking I did not know from which direction it was coming from but I heard it then it got nearer and nearer I could not come out of the shelter as I would have been seen by who ever it was the next thing I knew there were torches shone into my face it was the police once more they asked me if my name was Abigail I did not know what to say I just looked at them I think they knew by my face it was me so once more I was taking to the police car and took back to my parent house I was more or less frog marched up my garden path once again my father answered the door as usual once inside the house I was told to go into the kitchen while the police were with my parents in the living room about thirty minutes later I then heard them open the front door my mother came into the kitchen and I was waiting on the beating when she just told me to scrub the kitchen floor why she always got me to scrub the kitchen floor I will never know .

The next day I was on tender hooks waiting on the beating but it never came so what the police told my parents I will never know all I know was that it had stopped my parents hitting me that night I was sitting at the kitchen table with my brothers when I heard raised voices my brother David told me that my mother and father were fighting about me at this point I started to shake with nerves my mother came into the kitchen and she told me that I was to go up to my room and to wait up there as I walked out of the kitchen to go upstairs to my room I saw my escape the front door I just ran for it and as I got to the front door I could not get it opened as my parents had locked it my mother grabbed me from behind by my hair she dragged me up the stairs by my hair I was screaming and she just kicked my bedroom door open and she told me she would teach me one way or another to never run away again or tell stories ever again she threw me into the room and my father was standing there with the belt in his hand and as soon as I landed on the floor he started to hit me with the belt again the belt came raining down on top of me I was screaming in agony the neighbours must of heard my screams but the beatings kept coming then all of a sudden it stopped and he told me to go down the stairs and see my mother I don't think I felt anything at this point as I must have been in shock how else did I get down the stairs believe it or not my mother told me to do the dishes and then get to bed how I did the dishes was beyond me .

One night I was lying in my bed when I heard the door open and my father came to me and started touching me under the bedclothes and that's when I decided this must be my life and I must accept it as I had never experienced anything else just abuse my life carried on like this I came to accept it all then one day my mother started to shout at me for no reason she started calling me a slut and a tart and then she threw her cigarette lighter at me I remember it well it was a heavy lighter it bounced off my head then she told me to pick it up off the floor where it landed there was blood running down my face and I was crying she told me to shut up and that I was only looking for sympathy and I was shaking and she asked me what I was shaking for I was frightened to tell her as I did not want her to hit me again she told me I brought it on myself and that everything was my fault then she turned and walked out the door at the same time telling me not to say anything to my father about the cigarette lighter and how she had thrown it at me as she said that my father did not bother about me as I lay in bed that night I asked god to take me and to please not let me suffer any more as I just wanted peace in my life as I told him I really could not any more but it was not to be as the next morning I woke up in my bed wondering why god did not let me die .

The next day after breakfast my mother told me to go to the shops and get something for her I left the house and a neighbours daughter shouted on me and I walked up to her and asked what she wanted she asked me if I was alright as she heard my screams and that as far as she was concerned the whole street must of heard my screaming I told her as soon as I got the chance I was going to runaway for good this time as I had enough of the beatings she told me that she would go with me I told her it was up to her as I really did not know where I was going she told me she knew of somewhere to go and I asked where and she told me she knew of these two guys who shared a caravan and who worked with the circus as it was in town I thought anything was better than what I was having to put up with so we took a bus with my mothers message money and Shelley took me to the caravan to meet these two guys I was very shy in there company they asked me about myself I told them about the beatings but not the sexual abuse as I did not want them not liking me they told Shelley and I that they would hide us in the caravan until it was time for the circus to move on it just had another few days and then they were off to another town I could not wait so for once in my young life I felt free as there was no one to beat or hurt me I would of slept any where went any where just to get away from my parents and the beatings .

One day as my friend and I were sitting talking in

the caravan there was a loud knock on the door we did not answer it as we were told not to answer the door on any account until we heard them shout our names.

So we looked out of the caravan window and we saw these two policewoman standing with the guys who owned the caravan I totally hated them there and then as they had betrayed me after all I told them we knew we had to let them in as they already knew we were there as we opened the caravan door one of the police women took hold of me and she told me that I was going down to the police station my friend Shelley got taken into another car and I had to go into the another one . We arrived at the police station and the police woman told me to wait in a room she was away for about ten minutes then she came back into the room with my mother I could not look at my mother the police woman told me that she had a word with my mother and between them they had decided that I had to go for an examination I asked what kind of examination she told me an eternal I never had a clue what that meant so I was taken into another room and there was a couch and I was told to take my bottom clothes off and to lie down on the couch and while I was lying on the couch this doctor came in he told me what he was away to do at that point I just started to cry he was no very nice he shouted at me and told me to stop crying and to do as I was told and as this point I stopped crying and did as he told me put my legs up while he inserted this metal thing inside me he did what he had to do and then he told me to get dressed and then I was taken back into the adjoining room where my mother was she never said a thing to me she just looked at me I tried to read her face but I saw nothing after a while the police woman came in told me to wait outside while she spoke to me mother but while I was waiting outside the room there was another police woman I suppose that was to make sure I did not go anywhere a few minutes later my mother came out of the room with the police woman and then we walked to the police vehicle that was waiting on us when we got out of the station we were driven home the police woman walked with us to the door and then she left I tried to find out if my friend was about but my mother shoved me into the house .

When were in the house for about ten minute I felt as if I was waiting on a ticking time bomb to go off as there was no sound nothing just the noise in my head and the noise of my heart beating my mother walked into the front room and told me to come in there was no sign of my father when I walked into the room my mother told me to sit down and then she told me that the police woman had told her I was not a virgin and then she asked me who I had slept with I told her no one she called me a liar and that she had washed her hands off me and that no one will ever be interested in me as I was soiled goods then she told me to get to bed I was waiting on the beating to come but there was nothing I had past caring what happened to me at this point in my life just as long as they left me alone .

The next day my mother told me I was not going to school and that I was to stay inside the house I was just sitting in the living room when my father came in he told me to go upstairs I knew what was going to happen and again I ran to the front door and I opened it and ran down the path of the house but he got hold off me and dragged me back I was screaming as he dragged me back into the house and once the front door closed he started to punch me all over my body and up and down the hall then he told me to get to my bed as I was lying in my bed I started to think about what my mother said saying I was not a virgin well there was only one person to blame for that my father and to be honest I did not give a dam anymore I had past caring about me anymore I was kept off school after that beating as I was full of bruises and all sore I think my father knew he had gone to far this time with his beatings on me after episode I ran away again but I was always brought back to house and to my parent and to more beatings I took the beatings as well as the sexual abuse and every time they beat me I refused to let them see me cry but I did cry inside in fact I felt as if I was dying inside.

I left school to start work as a weaver in a local

jute factory I enjoyed my work but hated going home but what other choice did I have I worked hard each week and I handed every penny over to my mother she took all my wages from me she gave pocket money back and that was it she kept near enough all my wages and I was to frightened to say anything as I did not want any more beating I did not have many beatings after I started work but the sexual abuse did not stop after I had been working for about a month I was in the bath and my mother told me to hurry up as she needed a bath I told her I would not be long then she came into the bathroom and slapped me telling me not to answer her back I told her to leave me alone and then she pushed me under the water I could not get up as she was holding me down I was struggling to get up I was so afraid she was going to drown me then she suddenly just let go off me and she walked out of the bathroom I was so unhappy I did not want to stay there and with every feeling in my body I hated my mother and father more as each day past .

One night after work one of my friends came round and asked me if I wanted to go to her house to listen to her records I told her I had to ask my mother so I went and asked my mother but she said no so I walked to the door and told my friend I was not getting out and my friend told me I was fifteen and that they had to stop ruling my life and that I had to stand up to them so away I went back in and told them then they had no right to keep me in as I was old enough to do what I wanted regards going out well my father got of the chair and he hit me hard across the face by this point I told my father exactly what I thought of him and told him he was nothing but a bully well that was the wrong thing to say as he just keep hitting me and that night I got hit with a brush shaft I will never forget the pain I hobbled up the stairs to my room and I tried to look into the mirror but could not see out of my eye as it was totally closed I went to bed totally broken in body and in spirit I felt nothing for my parents but contempt I was surprised I slept but I did and I was awoken with my mother telling me to get up for work I told her I was all sore and my eye hurt she told me I was going to work no matter what I looked like .

As I went to the bus stop I was glad it was dark so that people could not see my face my friend Hazel was there and she asked me how I was as she said she heard me crying and screaming but she was frightened so she ran home I told her I understood she took one look at me in the street light and told me I looked terrible and that when we get to work then she would take me to see the personal officer as it was not right that my parents can do that to me so when we got to work Hazel took me straight to the personnel officer and she in turn took me to a social worker and she then took me to a doctor for an examination and it was my own doctor who seen me he never said anything to me he just wrote a few things down then the social worker took me in her car to some big house which I soon found out was an orphanage she told me as I was just fifteen I had to be under there care and that I was not allowed to go home to my parents .

I was told that I had to stay there for the time being I was so relieved to hear this I just burst out crying I was just glad that someone was on my side for once someone in authority actually took my side for once the social worker introduced me to the house parents and she then in turn handed me over to a girl who worked there she took me up some stairs which in turn led on to some bedrooms I was shown into this room with a few beds in it and a few sets of drawers it looked nice she showed me the bed that I would be sleeping in while I was staying there that night as I lay in that bed waiting on something to happen as when I was at home I don't think I ever slept deeply as I was always waiting and listening for my father to come into the room I never slept much that night as my mind was going round in circles and it was all about my past and the abuse sometime during the night I fell asleep but I had nightmares about falling down this tunnel and being trapped I was woken up by my house mother she told me that I would not be going to work but that I had to rest for the week to let my wounds heal the physical wounds and at breakfast I was told I was going into town in a couple of days when my bruises were not so bad to get some new clothes but first I had to go to the opticians to get glasses as my eye was damaged because of the punch my father gave me .

While I was in the orphanage I thought about my life a lot and what I had been through and I came to the conclusion that they were not my parents and that I must have been adopted as I never ever felt like I belonged there in that family I was an outsider I think it was my only way to cope with what they both did to me as I could not accept that as my true parents they could treat there own daughter that way I left my job at the jute factory and I got a job in a chemist just along the road from my parents house I Must have been working there for about a month when my big brother David came in for some thing for my mother when he saw me he gave me a smile and I gave him one back he asked how I was and I said I was doing fine I don't know if he ever told my parents I was working there as he never said I saw my brother a few times after that I was in the orphanage for about four or six months when I just left I took off I did not know where I was going I just wanted away the house parents were nice to me but I could not settle I was running away again so I hitchhiked all the way to Aberdeen and when I got there I found a social work department and I told them about my home town and about the physical abuse they manage to get me a live in job in a students hostel so once more I got settled I enjoyed my job I made a few friends by this time I never even thought about my parents or the life I had with them for once in my young life I was free to do as I wished and having some sort of normality in my life I was going out to night clubs at the weekends and I would got to the bowling during the week and it was here that I met up with the wrong crowd I would drink and stay out late and I would not get up for my work I had a few warnings from my bosses at the hostel but I did not care I suppose they were trying to help me but it was too late for me I did not care about them or me I wanted to be left alone I did not know what I wanted there was no direction to my life I suppose I was lost at that time in my life I was like a lost soul going from one place to another what was I searching for I did not know.

Things had came to a head one weekend I met up with my friends from the bowling and I never turned up for work I stayed out all weekend at my friends flat it never entered my head that my work bosses were worried about me I suppose I never ever had anyone to worry about me at in my life I went back to the hostel the following Monday and when I arrived there I was told that I had to report to my boss I was told from one of the other workers that I was in deep trouble I went along to the office and I knocked on the door I was told to come in and as I walked into the office I saw my social worker sitting there a Miss Turner she told me that my employers had terminated my employment as they could not be responsible for my well being any longer as I had enough warnings about my behaviour to be very honest I did not give a dam and I suppose the look on my face told them this and I was told that I was a very ungrateful girl as these people were only trying to help me I was told to go and get my clothes and belongings as Miss Turner was going to take me to some other place to stay for my own protection and as she said this I did not have a clue what she meant by protection I did not know who I had to be protected from.

So once again I was on the move I asked Miss Turner where was I going to she told me that I had to go into some sort of secure unit I asked what that meant she told me that I would not be allowed out and if I did go out there will always be some one with me as she did not trust me not to runaway I told her I was sorry also I told her that I was not happy at the hostel she asked me why I told her I did not know and I honestly did not know
.

We arrived at the home and it look just as she said a secure unit as there was bars on the windows and it look dull and dreary she kept hold of me when I got out of the car she rang the bell and the door opened and a man opened the door we were ushered into an office I was told I would be staying there temporarily until my hearing at some panel I asked Miss Turner what this panel was she told me the panel would decide my future for me I never gave it much thought after that I was taken to a bathroom by the house masters wife she told me to call her matron and that I was to have a bath and that she would give me some clean clothes after my bath I picked up my clothing and they looked more like boys clothes to me I asked the matron if I had to wear them she told me that this was the only clothes they had as the home was a boys home and that they sometimes took in girls on a short stay .

The matron showed me into a room and there I came face to face with six boys they were all about my age sixteen I was so embarrassed as I felt there eyes on me I did not know where to look I was told that this was the recreation room I just felt like running out of there but I had no where to go so I found a chair in a corner and I just sat down I did not know what to say or do then this boy came over and he spoke to me he was nice he asked me why I was there and I told him I ran away from my parents as they were always beating on me he said I more than likely will have to go to the children's panel I told him that I was waiting to go there he then told me that they will decide my fate he told me that a few of his friends went there and they never came back he then told me some of his friends ended up in borstal and others went to an approved school I asked him what kind of school is that he told me you can got there for years so I thought it could not be that bad at least it was a school not a home with bars on it as we were talking matron told me to come with her as it was time for bed she took me up some stairs and she showed me where I would be sleeping I never thought any thing about it until she told me that she was going to put the light out and lock the door I asked her why she was locking the door she told me it was because there was boys there so she locked the door and that was me until the next morning she came and let me out I did not like being locked up I hated it so for two weeks I was locked up at nights my social worker Miss Turner came and saw me a lot I liked her even though I gave her a lot of trouble

The day of my hearing at the children's panel came and my social worker took me into town we went into a big building and we were shown into this room and we were told to sit there until they read out my name as I sat there it came to me that someone in that room was going to decide my life for me so what the hell I thought who cares anyway we were sitting there a few minutes when some one came out of the room and shouted my name I though here we go I was told to sit down as Miss Turner was told the same they spoke to Miss Turner they asked her question about me and my family she in turn answered she told them that I ran away from them as my parents were beating on me and how she found me a job and how I did not last at the job after about twenty minutes later we were shown out of the room and had to wait another twenty minute as we sat there

I asked Miss Turner what was going to happen to me she told me that she did not know and that they were going to decide what was the best for me we were shouted back into the room as we entered the room I was told to sit down after a few discussions with Miss Turner I was told to stand up and that they the panel had decided that as my parents did not attend my hearing and that there was no one I could stay with and look after me then they had no option but to send me away some where for my own protection and that I would be sent to an approved school in Edinburgh for two years I looked at my social worker and she never said anything until we were out of the room she said she was sorry that I had to go away for two years she then told me that she would make arrangements for to take me the next day and that she would be driving me there herself I then thought I did not want put away for two weeks never mind two years then I thought it cant be that bad anything was better than being beat up by my parents and being sexually abused from my father.

The next day Miss Turner drove me to Edinburgh it was a very long journey one

hundred and five miles to be precise as she was driving I asked why they sent for my parents she told me that they the social work department had sent them the rail fare and that they did not turn up I was not surprised by this as I knew what they were like regarding me as there daughter they did not give a dam about me and they never would we eventually arrived at the approved school by the time we got there I was so tired and stiff after the long journey all I wanted to do was go to bed Miss Turner rang the bell and this woman answered the door she was a big woman she told us to come in we were shown into this sitting room and I was told to go and stand out side as there would be someone to come and collect me Miss Turner told me that she would keep in touch and that she would come and visit me sometime .

A few minutes past and this woman came through a door to the left of me and with her was another girl about my age the woman told me to go with the girl as she would show me where to go I asked where I was going and the woman told me I was going for a bath and to get cleaned up as we went through the doors the placed looked like a prison there was green paint on the walls it looked horrible as we were walking I asked the girl what the place was like she told me that it was not that bad she had been and seen worse she asked me how long I got I told her two years she told me she had been in there for a whole year and that she gets to go out into the town to buy records for the recreation hall and anything else they need I was shown in to this big room which held not one but three bathtubs they were massive the girl told me I must strip and get into one of the baths after my bath I was handed some clothes they were nothing special just a top and trousers after I was dressed I was taken to a big dormitory and shown my bed it was in a little cubicle she told me this was my living space it held a bed a little wardrobe and that was it after this she took me down some stairs and she took me to the recreation room and inside I saw that there was a lot of girls in there just like me dressed the same way some looked very hard and I knew there and then that I would have to be on my guard with them all but after a few days I found them to be the complete opposite they help me settle in and after about a week I was used to the place it was just as they said like a school but only difference was I lived there this was to be my home for the next two years .

During the day we went to classes and did chores and at night we would have to go to the recreation room we had no choice but to go to recreation room as we all had to be together and at night went we went to bed we were never locked in which I was glad of as I hated being locked in after about a month I noticed that at night a lot of the girls would share a bed and that sometimes they would be caught and then the staff would try and keep them separated at night there was a lot of lesbianism in that school but I suppose it had to be expected as there was no contact with the opposite sex apart from a Mr Simmons who worked at the school the female staff tried there best to curb such behaviour but they could never stop it as the girls would go away in pairs and hid in some corner where they could not be seen so there was a lot of bed hopping in there at nights .

The clothes that we had to wear were just terrible they were a bottle green and the uniform consisted of a green pinafore brown lace up shoes a green blazer and a green trench coat if it was raining I really hated that uniform.

I was there about six months when I was told from my social worker when she came to visit me that I was getting to go on a home visit I told her I did not want to go in fact I never ever thought about my home or family life I was not interested there was nothing there for me there any more my social worker told me that she went to see my parents and that they were willing for me to go home for the weekend and that they missed me and they wondered how I was doing at the school and she told me my mother was looking forward to seeing me well that was a shock my mother wanting to see me the person she beat up at every opportunity she got so after a long talk with Miss Turner I told her I was willing to go home for the weekend .

Friday came and I got ready to go home we were driven from the school by mini bus and some of the other girls were dropped off at there town one girl got dropped off near my home town I was next to be dropped off I had mixed feelings about this as I was going back after a years absence then when I started to think about my brothers and sister and I wondered how they had changed as for my parents I did not want to think about them maybe because they brought back to many bad memories for me I don t know as we drove across the Tay Road Bridge I started to get this weird feeling inside of me I don't know if it was fear or what but I know I never experienced it before as we drove into my street I told the care worker from the school that I was not feeling to good she told me that I will be fine and that she was going to have a word with my parents any way and that they would take me into the house so not to worry about any thing so I was eventually dropped off at my parents house by the member of staff who was with us she took me to my front door and she did not have to knock as the door opened and my mother stood there just looking at me and me at her I did not know what to say to my own mother Mrs Watson from the school had a word with my mother then I followed my mother into the living room as I walked in I saw my father and my brothers and sister they all looked different from what I remembered my father was sitting in the arm chair beside the fire he said hello I just said hi back this was my only communication with him all that weekend maybe he was ashamed of what he did to me I don't know my mother spoke to me and told me that I would be sleeping in the bottom bedroom with my little sister then she asked me if I was hungry I said no then I asked her if I could go and see my friend Hazel she said yes and to be back for my tea I ran out of the front door and went to Hazels house I knocked on the door and one of her sisters opened the door I asked if Hazel was in she said yes she told me to go in and she also said I look nice as I walked into there living room my friend Hazel was sitting there and she jumped up when she saw me she was so glad to see me just as I was so glad to see her to she told me that my father was fined for hitting me and that it was in the papers well some justice had been served as far as I was concerned my weekend went well I made some sort of communication with my brothers and sister and with my mother too but still I did not trust her she was civil to me I was always waiting on her shouting at me so before I knew it I was back on the road to the approved school .

It was after that weekend I missed my freedom and I wanted out to spread my wings again to be free once more so a few of us girls had decided that we would runaway so we planned where and when we should do it so one night we broke a window and we managed to squeeze out of the window and climb down a pole as our dormitory was high up.

.

There were six of us that night who managed to escape when we all got down the pole we ran out of the school grounds and as we had a local girl with us she told us she knew where there was a safe house after a lot of hiding here and there we made it to the safe house and in this house was an old man I could not believe my eyes as this girl about the same age as me sixteen started to kiss this old man I asked one of the other girls who was he she told me that he was her sugar daddy as I looked around the house it was not that clean but at least we were all free we stayed there for a few nights when one night there was a very loud knock on the door we just looked at each another and we knew that knock it was the police we were told to open the door or else they would open the door by force as there was nowhere to hid we knew we were caught the sugar daddy opened the door and the police came swarming in and they took us all back to the police station and we had to wait there until someone from the school came and picked us up a female member of staff and Mr Simmons the deputy came fifteen minutes later Mr Simmons looked very angry and once he got us into the mini bus he asked us all one by one why we run away they answered and when he asked me I told him I just wanted to he leaned over and he gave me one hell of a slap across the face and it hurt like hell I told him to piss off as he reminded me of my father when he hit me .

So when we arrived back at the school I was taken to a detention room and I was thrown in this little room and then I heard the metal door close behind me that's where I stayed for a whole week it was terrible I was locked in this little cell it consisted of a mattress on the floor with one blanket to keep you warm and a metal toilet they gave me my meals through a little drop down hatch in the door I hated it in there when I was allowed out of my little cell they gave me a letter which my mother had written to me and in it she told me that she had disowned me for running away I did not give a dam about her or what she thought as far as I was concerned if it was not for her and my father I would not have been in this place in the first place as they did not have the decency to come to my panel hearing .

I settled down once more at the school I was there about a year when I was told that I would be starting work at the local sweet factory with another girl from the school and we became very good friends her name was Mary we were working at the sweet factory for about three months when we were both asked to go to the principles office I wondered what we had done wrong I thought maybe the staff a the sweet factory had put a complaint in about us so off we went to see Mr Simmons my friend Mary went in first she was in there for about fifteen minutes then she came out I asked her what was going on but before she could answer Mr Simmons called me in as I went into the room Mr Simmons told me to sit down he then asked me what I would do if and when I get my release date I told him I did not know as I did not want to go back to my parents but what I did want to do was to join the army he told me that my release date would be coming up in a few months providing I kept out of trouble he then told me that I would be moving over to Heron house this was a little cottage in the grounds of the school this is where you went to prepare for your release date so my friend Mary and I moved over to Heron house that day we were so excited it was so different from the big school we both had our own room and there was also four other girls who stayed in the cottage who also went out to work too and there was two staff members whom we called house mothers so I was on my way out I could not wait and I knew I had to keep my nose clean because if I didn't I would have been back in the school again and no way was I going to upset the applecart so Mary and I were being prepared for our freedom .

As we were in Heron house we were allowed to go into town on Saturdays we were giving pocket money to spend how it was a good feeling to be able to walk out the school grounds and out the big gate and do what ever you wanted for a whole afternoon Mary and I were at Heron house for about three months when one afternoon after I got home from work I was told to go to the school to see Mr Simmons so after tea I went to see him he told me that my release date had come through and that I would be able to join the army if I wished and that I had made a wise choice he then arranged for me to go and see about joining up with the army I did the test that they give you and over the next few weeks I was given my medical which I passed then I was sent my joining up date and my train pass to get to Guilford training camp I was so excited about it all the day of my release I was sad to go as this had been my home for nearly two years and they did look after me well they were always there if you had a problem and they did there best to try and point you in the right direction regarding your life and to where you wanted to go.

So here I was about to embark on a new road and a new life I did not know what lay ahead of me but what I did know was that I am sure it would be exciting I was a bit apprehensive as I had the security of the school they fed me and looked after me for nearly two years and here I was on my own again.

I was driven to the railway station and dropped of at the pick up point I was told to look for a compartment with WRAC on it I climb aboard the train and I noticed that there were a few other recruits in there already they introduced themselves and I to them we all got talking they asked me where I came from I told them Edinburgh but I did not disclose about the school so once more I was on my guard as I did not want anyone to know about my past as far as I was concerned that was in the past and it would stay there we were all on a high by the time the train got to London so a few of us had decided to get a taxi to the pickup point and when we arrived at the pickup point there was an army bus waiting to take us to the barracks the ride on the bus was really exciting for me as I was my own and for once I was in charge of my own life so here I was on my way to Guilford training camp we eventually arrived at the camp and we were shown into this big building and we were all put into separate platoons then shown to our rooms the rooms held four girls at a time and after that we were shown into the mess hall were we were told to go and get something to eat I had never seen so much food before in my life after we had something to eat we were told to go back to our rooms and then we would see our platoon leader our platoon leader explained that we would be in there for six weeks and if we wished to leave after the six weeks then we were welcome to do so and if we decided to stay then we would be in the army for a few years .

So the next day our training began we were put into classrooms it was just like being back at school and in between class we were being fitted for our new uniforms I felt so proud when the day came when were handed our complete uniforms I put my uniform on in fact we all did and it felt good after our passing out parade we were allowed some leave so I went home with and English girl called Wendy as it was too far to travel to Scotland for the weekend as I had no where to go in Scotland it did not bother me one bit when I got back for my weekend I received some mail and as I opened the letters I found one from my mother as I read her letter it was with mixed emotions as in it she told me how things were at home and she asked me if I would go home on my next leave as she wanted to see me and that all my brothers and sister were missing me well that was a first I never had any one miss me before least of all my family so on my next leave which was a few months later I headed home to Scotland I got into my home town Dundee at three in the morning it was a long train journey and as I was crossing the Tay road bridge to Dundee I had so many mixed feelings I was sad frightened all at the same time as I was going back into the past and as the past held to many horrors for me I was in two minds whether to go to my parents house or get the next train back after I got off the train and after a lot of thought I had I decided to go to my parents house as I more intrigued about what they would say to me and most of all I wanted to see my brothers and sister as it had been a year and a half since I last saw them the last time was when I was home for the weekend from the school and a lot had happened since then also they had all moved to an new house so I gave the taxi driver the address and he dropped me off at my parents new home it looked smaller than the previous one I took my case from the taxi driver and I walked up the stairs leading to my parents house I was very apprehensive about approaching the door as I did not know what lay ahead of me in that door as I knocked on the door my mother answered she must have been waiting on me because it was very late and nearly four o'clock in the morning my mother looked different somehow she asked me if I had a nice journey I said yes it was fine then she made me a cup of tea she told me where my room was and that again I would be sleeping with my little sister Joan as I had travelled for a long time on the train I was totally knackered so after my cuppa tea I went straight to bed and I fell fast asleep .

The next morning when I woke up my sister had gone so I got up and went down the stairs and when I opened the door to the living room the first one I saw was my father he said hello I answered him then I saw all my brothers and sister they all looked different I suppose that had to be expected as they had got older and so had I as I was approaching my eighteenth birthday my week with my family went well I caught up with my brothers and what had been happening in there life I never mention much about my life in the approve school we mostly spoke about my life in the army and before in knew it I sitting on the train heading for Guilford in fact it was a most enjoyable week even though I was a bit apprehensive about staying with my parents and my father as I suppose the fear that he would come near me during the night never left me .

I was not long back at the barracks when I got that restless feeling again I wanted out I wanted away so once again I was on the road to self destruction I drank a lot at night I came into the camp totally pissed after being in town my work suffered I was put on a charge more often than not again I did not know why this happens to me I did not know what came over me all I know it happens and again after a few weeks I settle down again then before I knew it I was on home leave again and staying with my family and we had a nice night out and it was here that I met a guy his name was Peter and he was the son of one of my mothers friends he seemed nice he took me out bought me things he was really attentive to me he asked if he could write to me I said yes and he asked me to promise him that I would go out again with him on my next leave I said yes so I went back to the barracks and when I got my next home leave I saw a lot of Peter and we were a couple it was just before I was due to leave for Guilford that he asked me to marry him I did not even think about it I said yes as here was someone who loved me I never had someone love me before and I loved him well I had these feelings for him so it must be love so off I went to Guilford told them I was getting married and the next thing I knew I was a married woman living in my own home with Peter I was happy so very happy.

PETER

We were married for about two weeks when I was on my hands and knees cleaning the bedroom floor when Peter came in and asked me to make him something to eat I told him to do it himself as I was busy I just got the words out of my mouth then I felt this hard slap across my face I in turn picked up this heavy light shade made of glass and I threw it at him the light shade shattered into a million pieces at his feet he came across got me by the throat and told me never ever try that again as he would beat me up real good the next time then he told me that I was his and that I will do what ever he says as I belonged to him I told him to piss off and that I do my own thing and that I don't belong to him that's when he really got angry with me he hit me all over apart from my face I was in complete agony by the time he was finished with me as I lay there crying and in pain he told me to get to bed as he wanted sex I told him I did not want to do it he got hold of my hair and he more or less dragged me to bed then he tore my clothes off and he had sex with me then after he was finished he told me to get up and make him something to eat I did as I was told and I did not want any more beatings as I was too sore to argue with him after I gave him something to eat he told me that he was sorry for hitting me and that he would never do that to me again .

I believed him until the next time when we had no money due to his gambling on the horses he told me to go and ask his mother for money I asked him why he did not go he told me because I am telling you to go and then he hit me again he gave me a fly punch in the arm he took me to his mothers house and he told me to get in there and get some money and not to come out without any or else he will hit me again so I did as I was told and when I knocked on his mothers door she asked me what I wanted I told her that her son had sent me for to borrow some money off her she asked me what he had done with his own money I told her the truth she then asked me where he was I told her just along the road she told me to go and get him I did as I was told and as I approached Peter he asked me where the money was I told him he had to go and see his mother as she would not give me any money for him he asked me what I said to his mother I told him I told her the truth about him gambling on the horses he then told me I should of kept my mouth shut about his gambling we turned and walk back to his mothers house as we went in he told me to wait in the kitchen I heard Peter talking to his mother then a few minutes later he came out he told me we was leaving he looked angry he told me to get out then he said something to his mother and on the bus ride home he never said a thing to me I tried to talk to him but he just told me to shut up I looked out of the window of the bus all the way home I dared not look at him as our stop approached he took my arm and led me down stairs from the bus he kept hold of me all the way to our flat as he inserted the key in the lock he opened the door and threw me inside the door I asked him what was wrong and he told me that I never ever tell his mother what goes on between us as it is nothing to do with her and that our life was private and not to tell any one our affairs and then he gave me a few slaps on the face me up then after he hit me he told me to go and get undressed and go to bed we had sex and after the sex he told me that it was my own fault that he hit me as I made him angry and that I had better do as I was told or else I would come off the worse ever time and he was right I did come of worse so I stopped fighting him at this point also his gambling got worse and worse things got so bad we were evicted out of our flat as he spent the rent money as we had no where else to go so his mother took us both in .

His mothers said we could stay there just as long as she got her board money and I help around the house we were staying there for about a month when I had my first fight with his mother she asked me to make her a cup of tea and I told her she would have to wait as I was busy cleaning the bedroom that Peter and I occupied she then told me that I was there to help her around the house and that I should be grateful that she let me stay in her house I told her if it was not for her son and his gambling we would still be in our flat and also that I was not there to run after her and her whims as I had forgotten about the argument by the time Peter came home as he had been away collecting his dole money as soon as he stepped into the living room his mother started to run me down in front of him as Peter listened to his mother he gave me one of his looks and then he told me to get up the stairs to our room as he wanted to talk to me in private as we went up the stairs he gave me a shove and once in our bedroom he punched me in the back and he told me that I have to do as his mother tells me or else he would get angry I told him I was not going to slave for any one most of all his mother as I had enough of that while I was staying with my own parents years ago he then grabbed me by the throat and told me that I was going to do as I was told or else I would get a beating from him I was crying by the this time and I was shaking very badly I told him I was going to bed as I could not face his mother as I was too upset and my throat hurt he told me I was going no where but down the stairs to see his mother and when I got down there I had to asked his mother if she wanted a cup of tea so I had no option but do as he said when I walked into the living room his mother just looked at me I was sure she was smirking as she must of heard us arguing and she must of heard Peter telling me that I had to do as his mother said and as I looked at her I never saw her standing there I saw my mother as she reminded me of my mother and how she used to treat me like a skivvy .

I knew I had no choice but to do as she told me as I knew Peter would really hit me if I disobeyed her in any way so my life living with Peters mum was not any better than staying with my parents as I was cook cleaner bottle washer all in one go we stayed with his mother for three months when we had an offer from the council offering us a new built house we moved into the new house a month later and I started work in a store in the town I enjoyed my work there as it got me away from Peter and his moods when I received my first pay packet he told me to hand him my wages

and he would pay the bills and buy the groceries I asked him for some money for myself so that I can buy toiletries and some makeup he said I was not allowed to wear makeup and that he would buy what we needed for the house then he told me that I did not have the brains to look after the house and that I was hopeless and that included in bed as well I was so hurt at these words I just cried he told me to stop crying or else he would give me something to cry about so I stopped crying on the outside but inside I was crying and in pain because I was trapped in this hopeless marriage and had no where else to go .

One day after I had got home from work he asked

me why I had not pressed his trousers as he was going out that night I told him I forgot he then took hold me and started to hit me telling me I was hopeless then he went into the kitchen cupboard and came out with a plastic washing line rope and he hit me across the back with it I screamed as the rope came in contact with my back I pleaded with him to please stop he told me to beg for mercy I could hardly talk because of the excruciating pain in my back and over my body and I was sobbing my heart out at this point so he shouted at me once again to beg for mercy so I pleaded with him to stop and he did how I managed to get the words out of my mouth I never knew as my teeth was chattering after he stopped beating me with the rope he helped me up and then he took me to the bathroom and help clean my wounds I was a mess there were weals all over my back and body after he cleaned me up he help me to my bed and he made me a cup of tea as he handed me the cup I could hardly hold the cup as I was shaking all over and I was so cold he then went round to his side of the bed and then he started to undress I was just looking at him when he got into bed he started to fondle me I just wanted him to leave me alone and then he started to make love to me but inside I was screaming and screaming inside my head I went somewhere else after the screaming stopped in my head because the next thing I knew it was morning.

The following morning I was crying with the pain

but I could not cry out loud I had to do it inside I was relieved when Peter told me I was not going back to work he let me lie in bed all that day and for the whole of that week he was nice to me .

This did not last long as a few weeks later we were in town and we met a few friends of ours and they asked us to meet them at the pub that night I told them we did not have any money and that I was not working any more so they said that they would lend us some money Peter said that would be fine so we went home and agreed to meet them at the pub as I got dressed to go out Peter shouted on me and I went through to the room and he asked me what was this showing me the back of his shirt I did not know what he meant he told me that his shirt had a crease in it I told him I would iron it again he said don't bother as we are not going out any where that night as I was that hopeless I could not iron his shirt properly he then told me to go down the stairs and get his cigarettes as I was on my way down the stairs I saw the house keys hanging out of the front door I took the keys out very quietly as I could and I opened it and I closed it very quietly and I locked him in the house and then I ran as fast as I could where I was running to I did not know as all I knew I had to get away from him I came across some lockups and I crouched down behind them I hid there for about fifteen minutes when all of a sudden I heard this noise behind me it was Peter before I had time to run he got hold of me and he punched me in the eye then he dragged me all the way home screaming and kicking all he kept saying was wait till I get you home he had my arm up my back so that I could not run and when we got home he locked me in and he threw me down the stairs I landed at the bottom of the stairs in a heap and he jumped down them two at a time and he dragged me into the living room and he beat me again with the rope and he kicked me as I lay curled up on the floor and after he was finished he dragged me up the stairs and he ripped my clothes off and started to have sex with me after he was finished I got up and went to the bathroom to have a look at what damage he had done to me I could not see out of my eye and I had a few bruises on my face and my lip was cut inside and it was swollen .

After that night he would not let me out of the house for a month he locked me in each time he had to go somewhere he would not even answer the door to his mother as I heard her shout through the letterbox one night and as she shouted he told me to keep quiet or else he would punch me so we sat there listening to his mother hollering through the letter box we were in that house for about two years when we had to move again as he had ran up a lot of debts and we could not afford the repayments so once again we had to move into his mothers house once more I was sitting in my bedroom at his mothers house and I looked into the mirror the person that looked back at me was not me nothing like I was when I married Peter I was so skinny he had made me into a nervous mental wreck and as he always told me if I ever left him he would find me and he would kill me as I belonged to him .

We were married about two years when he started to go out and have affairs we were still with his mother and every Friday night he would go out and at times he would not come home or else he would come home stinking of perfume I was to frightened to say anything to him so I put up with it even though I was totally devastated that he had found other woman more desirable than me but at the same time I always remembered what he said I was hopeless in bed.

One day as I was sitting in the house with his mother a knock came to the front door she told me to go and answer it as I opened the door the police were standing there they asked me if Peter lived there I said yes and then they told me that he was in the local police station on theft charges I told them to come in and his mother asked them what they wanted they told her what they told me and that Peter was up at court the next day so the next day his mother and I went to court and when it was his turn in front of the sheriff to be sentenced we heard that he had broken into a house and was caught the sheriff sentenced him to six months in a young offenders institution .

STRENGTH FROM WITHIN

While he was in the institution my relationship with his mother got a bit better as she told me that Peters father was just as bad as Peter regarding the beatings and that's why she divorced him on the grounds of cruelty I just looked at her when she said this as she knew how bad things were regarding my marriage to her son I knew that I should leave him but where would I go plus he told me he would kill me if I ever left him I really believed he would if he ever caught up with me I would go and see Peter in the institution and he always promised me at every visit that he would never hurt me any more when he got out as he had thought about what he had done to me over the past two years and told me he loved me very very much and asked me to forgive him so I did .

The day had come when Peter was due for release and he got home very early I was still in bed when he came into the room I felt the bedclothes being pulled from me I sat up half sleeping and asked what was going on as soon as I saw Peter standing there I knew something was wrong he then asked me where I got to at the weekends I told him no where and that I only went to bingo with his mother at the weekends he asked me if I ever went on my own I said just once he then told me that I was with someone on that weekend I told him I did not know what he was talking about he told me some one that he knew wrote to him and told him that I had been with some other guy when he was locked up in there I told him they were lying he asked me if I was calling his friend a liar I said yes he then slapped me hard across the face then he started to call me all the sluts under the sun I was crying and he told me to shut up and he punched my arm the next thing the bedroom door opened and his mother was standing there she told Peter to leave me alone and what was going on he then told her what someone had written to him while he was in the institution she told him it was all lies and when I went to the bingo on my own I was home for nine thirty and I was definitely not out on the town as his friend suggested he then turned around and said he was sorry then his mother left the bedroom and he came and lay beside me he then asked me if I missed him I said yes even though I knew it was the latter as I was so afraid of him no that's an understatement I was petrified of him and deep down I think he knew this as I always had to give him the answers he wanted to hear .

A few weeks after he came out of the institution we were offered a house again from the council it was a multi story block and the house that we were offered was thirteen flights up it was a nice house so Peter said that we would take it our life carried on as usual he was still beating me and he was still going out and leaving me in the house plus he always locked me in I could never get out as we had no phone I had no way of getting in touch with any one so I had to sit and wait until he came home before I could get out my life was going to the shops and back again with Peter I had no social life of my own and what social life I did have Peter would always be there I was a prisoner in my own home I used to cry with despair .

One night Peter had been out drinking it was the weekend and he brought some couples back with him as I was in bed he gave me a shake and told me to get up and make some sandwiches for his guests I got up and did as he told me they sat drinking for a long time it was six a clock in the morning when they all left I was so tired by this time and I told Peter I was going to bed he told me I did not go to bed until he told me and he made me sit there until he said it was ok for me to go to bed and when I got to bed I just got lying down on the bed when Peter asked me what I was doing I told him I did not understand what he meant and he told me that I was a dog and where do dogs lie I told him on the floor and he told me to get out of the bed and lie on the floor I did as he told me and I lay on the floor with one cover over me he would not let me into the bed that was my first of many nights that I slept on the floor there were times when I was so tired I just wanted to sleep but Peter would not let me he told me I did not sleep until he told me I was like a zombie by this time I was his puppet he pulled the strings I moved I was so afraid to move or say anything in case it made him angry. .

It was a Sunday night and Peter told me to make him some supper while I was making it he told me to hurry up I knew that tone in his voice so I started to shake as I knew if I did not hurry up he would come through and give me a thump and sure enough he came through and asked me what was taking me so long I told him I was waiting on the kettle to boil he then turned round and opened the kitchen window and he got hold of me and then he picked me up and he pushed me half out of the window I was screaming at this point god I thought I was going to die I actually thought he was going to kill me then he hauled me back in from the window and just walked away he never said a thing he just picked up some supper from the kitchen top and walked back into the living room as for me my heart was racing and I was crying no I was sobbing my heart out I wanted away from him before he killed me I sat on the kitchen floor huddled in the corner a total nervous wreck trembling then he came into the kitchen and told me to get up and to get undressed there and then as he wanted sex and he took me there and then on the kitchen floor then he got up and told me he was going out and that he wanted his clothes pressed with no regards to me he was one sick sadistic bastard and how I hated him and loved him at the same time.

Once again we had to leave that house he told me that he found us a flat in the town as it was nearer his drinking pubs and it would save him from getting a taxi home all the time so we settled in this flat then things changed for me I never got locked in any more I was allowed to go to the bingo on my own as it was just across from our flat but I had to go straight home for Peter coming in where Peter went and what he did I did not know as he never told me and at the weekends sometimes he would stay out all night I knew he was with someone but I got passed the hurt and the pain with his womanising I was used to it what else could I do also I did not have any friend my life consisted of just the two of us as Peter made sure of that my life carried on as usual until one day I was out shopping when this woman stopped me and asked me where I got my shoes from I told her my husband bought me them she told me that there were hers as she had dyed them and that the original colour was black so the next thing I knew I was charged with handling stolen goods you see Peter always bought my clothes and shoes so he must of broken into some ones house and stole them I felt so ashamed .

Peter told me that I had to plead guilty to house breaking because if he did then he would be jailed and as it was my first offence nothing would happen to me so on the day of the court case I pleaded guilty to theft and house breaking the judge gave me six months in a women's prison I just turned round and looked at Peter as I was being led down to the cells he just shrugged his shoulders I was totally shocked so here I was on my way to jail to spend the next six month locked up again for something I never done I took the rap for him and where did it get me I was still in shock when I had to spend my first night in Perth prison in a holding section for women until I could be transported to Greenock women's prison the next day .

I arrived at Greenock prison early in the morning with a few other prisoners and as we were driven through these big gates I started to feel so nervous as here I was about to be locked up again we were shown into this reception area then they asked me my name and then they told me to sit in this little box cubicle and to get undressed and I was told to put on the clothes that they said was sitting on the bench inside after I put the clothes on I was led through to this other room and then they took me through a locked gate and I was taken up these metal stairs to my cell that was going to be my home for the next six months as they locked me in my cell I just sat on my bed and wondered how my life came to this I did not feel anything I did not cry I don't think I had any more tears left or was it the fact that I was free of Peter for six months and no more beating I don't know as I lay there on my bed listening to the noises of the other inmates and the metal doors banging my cell door opened and two other inmates came in I was not sure as what to say or do they asked me my name and asked me what I was in for I told them these two women who were called Carol and

STRENGTH FROM WITHIN

Jean and they were to my saviours during my time I was in prison there were good to me regarding smokes and toiletries until I got my first wages I was assigned to the laundry room that was to my work place for the next six months and all the other woman were really nice at least I was able to laugh in there more than what I did when I was with Peter.

I wrote to Peter as often as I could but I never got any replies to my letters and that hurt me also he never came to see me either and that upset me even more my cell mates told me to forget about him when I get out because if he really loved me he would of written to me or came to see me I knew they were telling the truth but I loved him why I loved him I did not know as all he ever did to me was beat me and belittle me all the time .

There was always a glimmer of hope that he would write or come and see me I was nearing my release date and still no letters from him by this time I was totally confused and angry that he could do this to me after all I had did for him taking the rap for him it should have been him locked up as it was his crime not mine I had been a fool I was a fool .

A week before I was due to be released I received a letter from Peter and in the letter he explained that his mother had taken ill and that as there was no one to take care of her and he had to do it I did not believe this for one minute but there was nothing I could do while I was inside these prison walls because knowing Peter he had been up to no good .

The day of my release came I was out of that prison and back in Dundee by nine o'clock and as I stepped of the train I saw Peter as I got nearer him I started to feel anxious and inside I was shaking inwardly I felt as if I could not breath when I eventually got up to him he asked me how I was I told him fine then I asked him what was going on and what was the real reason he did not write or come and see me he then told me he will tell me when we got to my parents house I told him I did not talk to my parents he told me he had sorted everything out with them and that they wanted to see me I then asked him what was so important that after all these years my parents had decided they wanted to see me then he told me to just and wait till we got there and then I will find out everything I was very curious at this point wondering what the hell was going on so we walked to my parents house I was just about to put my foot on the first step to climb the stairs when Peter told me to wait a minute as he had to tell me something I turned and looked at him and then I got the truth he told me he had met someone else while I was in prison and that was the reason he did not write or come and see me in prison I was gutted here was the man who beat the living daylight out of me every chance he got made my life a total misery for nearly three years made me do a prison sentence for him and he stands there and tells me he has met someone else I could not say anything as I watch him walk away from me I was in shock so I walked up the stairs to my parents house with a very heavy heart as it was breaking and there was nothing I could do about it all.

As I knocked on my parents front door my mother opened the door and she told me to come in as soon as I got inside the house I started to cry I don't know if it was the fact this was the first time I saw my mother in a few years or the fact I had just been dumped by my rat of a husband my mother told me that Peter was seen going about with a woman and that as far as she knew the woman had a flat not far from my parents house how could he do that to me and at that precise moment I hated him loathed him and loved him at the same time my emotions were all in a turmoil for the first time in my life my mother hugged me as I was breaking my heart she told me she never did like Peter as she heard so much stories of what he was like and how he beat me she told me even though we never spoke she still wondered how I was doing she told me she was hurt to hear I was in the jail and I told her the real reason I was in the jail she told me I would better just forgetting about him as far as I was concerned that was all I wanted to do but I knew I never would as I loved him he was part of me no matter what he did to me .

My mother told me I could stay there if I wanted to I told her I had no where else to go and that I had no other clothes but what I was wearing she told me Peter handed in all my belongings in to her a few months back when he gave up our flat .

After I shed a lot of tears I decided that I had to find out all about this woman that Peter was with I asked my mother if my old friend Carol was still in her old house she said yes so I went in search of Carol when I found Carol I asked her if she knew any thing about this woman Peter was with she told me she had seen them about but that was all I told her I had to find out where Peter and this woman stayed as I wanted to see what she looked like my friend Carol said that I should just forget about them and just get on with my own life I told her I could not do this till I found out where the two of them were staying and what was so special about this woman he had taken up with so Carol and I went in search of Peter and his fancy piece after knocking on a few doors we eventually found them they stayed in a flat two stairs up in a tenement I knocked on the door and my friend Carol stood in front of the door in case Peter answered it as I did not want to face him but I knew I had too no matter what as the door opened this woman asked Carol what did she want Carol told her she wanted to talk to Peter she said he was not in then I stood in front of Carol and I recognised her straight away she was the girlfriend of one of Peters friends her name was Kim Vale I asked her if she recognised me she said yes I asked her what happened to Allan Smart who was Peters friend she told me she dumped him when she started to go out with Peter I asked her why she went chasing a married man she told me Peter done all the chasing and that she wanted nothing to do with him knowing he was married but Peter would not leave her alone and that Peter said he was finished with me and had been for months I told her that I was in the jail for six months she told me she never knew this then she tried to close the door I stopped her and I told her to tell Peter to meet me at my parents house the next day and to tell him if he did not come I would be back tomorrow I felt like tearing her hair out by the roots but I knew better than that as I was not going to give Peter the satisfaction of giving me any more beatings as I knew if I touched her he would touch me .

That night as I lay in my bed at my parents house and I could not sleep as all I thought about was Peter and that Kim Vale together and the more I tried to push it out of my mind the more it came back to haunt me I eventually got up made myself a cup of tea and I did a lot of thinking about my life with Peter and after a lot of thought I decided every one was right I was best to forget about him even though I was hurting I knew I had to get away so instead of waiting to see if Peter would turn up I went and applied for a job out of Dundee as I knew I had to get right away from Peter and Dundee if I was going to move on without him as I really did not want to bump into him and Kim every day as they just lived around from my parents house .

I started my job a few days later it was in a hotel in Perthshire I was in training for to be a silver service waitress after a few months I left that job as I got that wanderlust feeling back so I phoned up for another job in a small care home in Dunoon so once again I was on my travels I liked my job there at the care home again after a few months I decided it was time I went home to Dundee as the thoughts and feeling I had for Peter were not as bad as what they were when I first left Dundee so I wrote to my mother and told her I was coming home and if it would be ok to stay with her she wrote back saying that would be fine.

I was staying with my parents when I applied for a job in a local jute factory and I started working there as a weaver after a few weeks I was getting on with my life my relationship with my parents was getting better there was no more hassle from them and I got on well with my brothers and my sister it was 1974 and I was twenty one by now and I never saw Peter or mentioned him at last I was over him.

At the weekends I would go out with a few friends

and we would go to the local parlour for a dance and a carry on and we had fun one night while we were there a friend of Peters came over to me and asked how I was doing I told him I was fine and just getting on with my life the best I could and as I did not want to open closed wounds I did not even mention Peters name I did not want to know what he was up to I would not let myself think about him so I left it at that but Peters friend George Henderson kept going on about Peter I told him I was not interested and that we were finished he then told me that Peter was really broken up when he heard I left Dundee I told him that he was with Kim so why was he broken up he then told me that as long a Peter knew where I was he was happy but with me going off like that he was in a panic because he did not know what I was up too .

When I got home I tried to make sense of what George Henderson told me about Peter why was he so interested in me when he was with Kim then as I could not find any answers I eventually fell asleep the next day I was sitting eating my breakfast when there was a knock at the door my mother answered the door she then shouted on me telling me there was someone at the door and when I looked to see who it was it was shocked to see that it was Peter standing there I asked him what he wanted he told me he had to see me I told him I was not interested he then told me the he saw George Henderson what he really meant was that George Henderson saw him as I had a hunch that George would go and see Peter to tell him I was home Peter asked me to meet him somewhere that night I asked him if he was still with Kim he said yes but they were just living together but not sleeping together I did not believe this so I told Peter I was not interested so the more I refused to see him the more I could see that he was getting angry he then took hold of me at the door and looked straight into my face I thought he was going to hit me so I tried to step back he told me that I was his wife and that he was never ever going to let me go and if I ever went with any one else he would kill me then he let me go turned and walk back down the stairs I was shaking by the time I closed the door my mother asked me what was wrong I told her what Peter said she told me that he was just angry that I never gave into his demands and that through time he would get the message that I was not interested in him any more I realised my mother was right so I just got on with my life .

As I never heard from Peter again I took it for granted that he had decided to leave me alone but one day as I was walking home from work and as I past a block of flats this hand came out and grabbed me I screamed and this hand went over my mouth I tried to turn round to see who it was then I recognized the voice telling me to be quiet it was Peters voice and when I went quiet he let me go I asked him what did he want from me he told me that he wanted me back and that he was finished with Kim I asked him if he really meant that he said yes he then asked me to meet him that night in a bar in the town I told him yes just to get rid off as I was afraid of what he would do to me if I said no.

I never mentioned any of this to my parents as I did not want to bring any trouble to there door and the more I thought about it I knew I had to meet Peter or else there would be trouble if not just for me but my parents as well so I met Peter at the pub we agreed to meet in he told me that he never thought I would show up but was glad I did after he bought me a drink I asked him about his relationship with Kim and what went wrong he told me that he had went off her and things had got really bad regarding his relationship with his mother as she had never forgiven him for leaving me in prison without a letter or a visit I was shocked to hear this as Peter and his mother were close he then asked me to go back with him then he said that after all the years we had been together it must count for something I told him I did not have a life and that he was always beating me just because things were not going his way and that I could not go back to that again he told me he had changed and he would never treat me like that ever again as he knew what he had lost when I got those jobs out of town he told me he was frantic as he did not know where I had gone to I thought this was a different Peter the old Peter wound not have opened up and admitted that to me in the past so before we knew it last orders and been called so we left the pub and as Peter walked me home to my parents house he told me that he would be in touch very soon and then he left me at the bottom of the stairs leading to my parents house.

I never saw Peter all that week so on Saturday my friends and I had decided to go out dancing that night we went to the dance hall we were having a nice time dancing away when all of a sudden I was swung round and there facing me was Kim I asked her what the hell was she playing at she told me to leave her Peter alone I told her that I was not after Peter and that he was after me she told me I was a liar and that Peter had told her that I wanted to see him then all of a sudden she ripped my blouse right down the middle just as well I had a jumper on under it we started to fight on the dance floor then a few bouncers came and separated us my friends told the bouncers how Kim just ripped my top so Kim was put out and I went down the stairs with my friends to clean up as we were coming out of the toilets this hand grabbed me I looked and it was Peter I told him to go away and get Kim as she was waiting on him outside he told me he was not interested in her only me I asked him why he had told Kim all those lies about me and how I was chasing him not the other way round he then all of a sudden he asked me if I was going to go back to him I said no as he was still with Kim he then thumped me right in the eye I was screaming and someone came and put him out I could not believe that he had came to the dance with Kim then ask me to go back with him and because I said no he thumps me.

I was so hurt and angry at Peter and Kim and most of all myself as I sat in that pub the other week and like a fool I believed everything he told me regarding his relationship with Kim my friend Carol asked me if I wanted to go home I said yes as my eye was really sore and so was my feelings I phone my younger brother Robert and I told him what Peter had done to me he told me that I had to stay where I was and that he would come and get me and he would walk me home I waited fifteen minutes then Robert came into the dance hall he asked if I was ok I said I was fine apart from the sore eye as we walked out into the night Robert told me that Peter was waiting on me at our parents house I asked him what he meant he told me that Peter had managed to get round my mother and tell her that he was so sorry for hitting me in the eye and that he just got angry because I would not go back to him and apparently he promised to never ever hit me again as my mother told him that he cant just lift his hands to me when ever things don't turn out the way he wants them he told my mother he knew that and that he loved me and that he never stopped loving me my mother said he had a funny way of showing it.

When Robert and I went into the house my mother

was there so was Peter I asked where my father was my mother told me he had gone to bed then she told me to come and sit down as I sat down she told me that Peter and I had to sort out our differences I told her I was really fed up getting hit for nothing and that Peter was still with Kim but Peter denied this and told me he had been away from Kim for a few weeks I did not believe him my mother then told me that Peter had promised her that he would never hit me again if we got back together and she told me that Peter really loved me and she thought I should give him another chance I could believe my ears I just looked at Peter and he gave me a smile my mother then told me Peter was staying with us until he could get us a flat as she said this she told me that we could sleep on the sofa bed in the living room I told her I was not sleeping with him and she then turned around and told me I was and that Peter deserved a second chance just like any one else so that was it I had to sleep on that sofa bed with Peter that night I was having my life ruled for me once again and I just had to put up with it.

As I lay next to Peter that night he promised me the earth but I was not that stupid and I had this daunting feeling about me so once again we were a couple after few days of this so called married bliss my mother asked me how we were getting on I told her that I this feeling inside of me that Peter would be off and away back to Kim she told me not to be daft and that any one can see that he loved me I told her it remains to be seen to see if he could keep all the promises that he made to me that first night he stayed with me at my parents house .

We were together for about a month when one day I came home from work and my mother told me that Peter had went out to go flat hunting and that he never came back I told her he was away flat hunting alright as he was away back to the flat he shared with Kim I just knew this as I told my mother I knew Peter and that he was nothing but a dirty snake and a bloody liar and that he would never change and that he had used me and my parents and as I warned my mother previous that this would happen and sure enough a few days later I saw them both together and as far as I was concerned they were to close to my home that I decided to move in with a friend of mine as I did not want to keep bumping into Peter and Kim every day of my life as I had enough of him and her to last me a life time .

I change my job as I did not want Peter jumping out at me on my way home and I changed my address I moved in with my friend Carol and her husband Ronald and I got on with my life once more I was staying with Carol when I met this guy called Terry Brown but that relationship never got off the ground as he had a hang up about his ex-wife and that no one as far as he was concerned could come up to her expectations so he got told to head I could not be bothered with that crap in my life as I had enough crap from men to last me a lifetime .

One night as I was walking home from visiting my parents I was grabbed from behind and I knew right away who it was as I could smell that distinctive smell he had about him it was Peter I asked him to let me go and to please leave me alone he told me that he would never leave me alone as I was part of him just as he was part of me I told him to go back to Kim as I had about all I could take from him and his sick ways he told me he had left Kim as he could not stop thinking about me I told him if he love me that much he would never of went back to Kim when he was staying with me at my parents house he then told me Kim had taken an overdose and that she needed taking care of as she was just a weakling and she needed him to survive I asked him why he was not with her if she needed him that badly all he said was she would get over it that was Peter all over not a care in the world about any one but himself he then asked me to go back to him so to keep the piece I asked him where were we going to stay he told me he was back with his mother and that he had told her he was going to see if I would come back to him and that we could stay there I told him to let me think about it then he asked me to go back to him there and then I played for time I told him I had to get my clothes he then said he would come with me I did not know what to do as this point I then told him I could not just go into Carols house and tell her I was leaving just like that as she and Ronald had been good to me he agreed with me so we made arrangements to meet up the next night and that I would have my clothes with me he told me that if I did not show he would come and get me as he knew where I stayed and that he would cause so much trouble for me and my friends that they would end up throwing me out so what choice did I have I could not see my friends hurt in any way so the next night I went back to Peter to live with his mother once more.

My life with Peter and his mother was fine he kept his promise and he never hit me he still had a temper when things did not go his way but he did not hit out at me as I found the reason being his mother had told him if he ever lifted his finger to me while we were staying with her she would get the police and that she would go witness to the assault well at least his mother was on my side for once and I was glad of it as she seemed to keep Peter in check after we stayed with his mother about two months Peter told me that he had the chance of a little holiday hut and it was going for rent I asked him where this holiday hut was he told me it was somewhere called the Downs I asked where this was he told me not far from Dundee as we could get a bus to there I asked him what I was going to do for work he told me I did not need to go to work any more as he would look after me and provide for me so once again we were on the move we got on the bus to the Downs I did not have a clue where we were heading as the bus took us out into the country as I was looking at the scenery Peter told me to get up as we were near the Downs the bus stopped in the middle of nowhere and we got off the bus Peter took the cases we walked through all these holiday huts until we came to a little hut Peter took out a set of keys and he opened the door and when stepped inside I was shocked as it was just like a house it had a bedroom and a living room and a little kitchen it was very cute I asked where the toilet was he told me that we had an outside toilet I screamed at him what do you mean an outside toilet he told me we had a portable one that you emptied yourself I could of cried what had I let myself in for then I noticed there was no light switches and I asked Peter how do we get light when it gets dark he told me that there was paraffin lights and that it would be ok then he told me that I had to cook on a gas cooker and that it was a portable one and that we had to use a bottle of gas I did not believe what I was hearing but I just kept my mouth shut .

A month had past and Peter was keeping his promise we shared the chores and at night it was so romantic just the two of us in this little hut and the glow from the paraffin light gave it such a cosy look .

One night as we were lying in bed there came a

knock at the door it was pitch black outside so I asked Peter to go and see who was there as I wondered who was out in the middle of nowhere at this time of night as I looked at the clock on the bedside table it read one in the morning I heard Peter talking and then I heard this female voice I got out of bed to see what was going on Peter tried to close the door but I was to quick for him and when I looked out into the darkness all I saw was a shadow but as my eyes became accustomed to the dark I saw Kim standing there I asked Peter what the hell was going on then he told Kim to come in I could not believe what I was hearing I told Peter that I was not staying there especially with Kim being in the same room as me he told me to be quiet as he would fix everything out he then told me he was going to fetch water from the well at the top of the field he then turned and told Kim not to move as he would see her when he got back with the water while he was away I asked her what did she want and how did she find out where we were she did not answer me so I walked over to her and told her to get the hell out of here and out of Peter and my life she started to cry I asked her why she was crying she told me that she loved Peter and that she would do any thing to get him back I just looked at her and I knew exactly how she felt she was sitting there in the exact position I found myself about a year ago when I came out of the prison.

Peter came in with the water and he made us all a

cup of tea then I asked him what was going on and why was Kim here he told me to be quiet and that he will fix things out with Kim I asked fix what out that's when he told me that Kim was staying the night I could not believe what I was hearing I told him I was not staying there with her in the hut he told me there was no buses at that time of the morning I told him I would walk back to Dundee he told me not to be stupid I then got up went back into the bedroom I had to get away and think how did she know where we were I could not understand it as Peter had never left my side but to sign on the dole and I was with him at all times an hour later Peter came into the bedroom and told me Kim was staying the night on the sofa in the living room here I was lying in bed with my husband and his girlfriend was lying through the next room I just could not believe how this all came about but I knew for sure I had to get out of this situation that I found myself in I felt like hitting him as he lay there beside me but thought better of it as I did not what to start him off in one of his moods Peter interrupted my train of thought by asking me to have sex I could not do this what with his girlfriend in the next room he told me Kim and he had finished months ago so I asked him again why was she here he just kept telling me he would sort things out the next thing I knew he dived on top me and started to have sex with me I just lay there as I could not bring myself to do it he told me to move myself or else he would just go next door to Kim as she would not push him away I did not know what I felt after he had finished I was just glad it was all over .

The next morning as I woke up Peter was not beside me I crept out of bed and I put my ear to the bedroom door I heard Peter and Kim talking I got very angry at this point so I yanked the bedroom door open and I asked the two of them what the hell was going on Peter told me to be quiet I asked him again when was Kim leaving because if she did not leave then I would as I had enough of his crap he walked over to me and told me I was not going anywhere as he told me he had taken my purse out of my bag when I was sleeping he then told me that I will do what ever he tells me to do or else I knew what he would do to me I went back into the room feeling defeated to get dressed when Peter came into the room he told me that I belonged to him and I was staying put and that I would never ever leave him again as he would make sure of it .

I had to stand up to him I had to show I was not frightened of him even though I was shaking inside I could not let him rule me anymore so I told him I would escape as soon as I found the opportunity he walked up to me and he gave me one hard slap across the face and he told me that he was the master and I was his slave to do his bidding no matter what that was when I released I had made one terrible mistake of ever going back to him and letting myself believe that he had changed for the better I refused to cry when he hit me I promised myself there and then that I would never show him how much pain I was in also as soon as I found the opportunity I was getting out of this place .

He then took hold of me by the arm and told me to get back into bed I did as he told me then he went back into the living room and I heard him talking to Kim a few minutes later he came into the room and he got undressed and came and lay down beside me he then asked me if I loved him at that point I did not know what I felt for him I was totally confused by it all I knew if I said I did not know he would just lash out at me so I had no choice but to say yes then he asked me if I would do anything for him to make him happy I said yes he did not answer for a few minutes then all of a sudden he shouted on Kim to come in I asked him what the hell did he want Kim for he told me to be quiet as the bedroom door opened there stood Kim with just her underwear on he then told me Kim was coming into bed with us and that we were all going to have some fun together I jump out of bed and I told him to fuck off I was not doing that for any man and then I shouted that I hated him and that was nothing but a fucking pervert he jump out of bed and he dragged me by the hair back to the bed and he told me that if I ever shout at him land like that again he would break my legs and arms and I knew he would keep his word .

STRENGTH FROM WITHIN

So I had no option but to get back into bed with Peter and Kim I was so hurt and angry at the way things had turned out Kim was told to kiss me and I was told to kiss her back I felt sick at the thought of it but I had no other choice Peter told us what to do and how to do it and when to stop and when to start again I don't know how long we were doing this when all of a sudden Peter slapped Kim and I across the face we just looked at him Peter then told us that we were ignoring him the truth was he could not handle the reality of how own fantasy .

This was my way of life for a few weeks until I had the opportunity to get the hell out of this situation I found myself in Peter had to sign on at the labour exchange and he told me and Kim that we were going with him and that he warned me not to try any funny business or else he would kill me as for Kim she was happy enough to do what he wanted just to keep him so he never had any problems with her that way so from the time we left the hut he kept a tight grip on me on the bus when we finally got to Dundee he kept his hold on me I asked him if I could go to the toilet he told me he was not falling for that excuse I told him that I would wet myself there and then if he did not let me go so he had no option but to let me go I made out I was going into the toilet then I suddenly changed direction and I ran like the wind to get away from him he chased me and I could hear him shouting that I could never escape him as he will find me in the end I ran through the town centre and I kept running till I could not run any more my heart was beating so badly I thought it was going to burst I found myself back at Carols once again I told her that Peter was back with Kim and that I could not take any more of his crap and how I had to get away because every where I go Peter finds me so I told her I could not stay with her as Peter would just hunt me down again .

I managed to secure a live in job in Dundee working as an assistant cook I was there about a month when my friend Carol came and saw me she told me that Peter had been at her door looking for me and that she told him I had a job out of town he told her he will find me no matter where I was I told Carol as long as he thinks I am out of Dundee he will not go looking for me she told me she was not to sure so once again I got on with my life the best I could as I put what happened in that hut right out of my mind it was if it never happened .

After my work had finished I liked to go and see my friend Carol as it gave me a break from where I worked and slept I would stay and talk to Carol until about ten at night I was coming out of Carols tenement when some one took hold of me I tried to scream but there hand was over my mouth I knew right away who it was Peter he let me go after I promised him I would not make a sound I asked him what he wanted I told him I was never ever going back with him and that he had Kim and

STRENGTH FROM WITHIN

I pleaded with him there and then to leave me alone he told me he never will as I belonged to him no one else he then told me that he knew where I worked and that if I did not go back to him then he would tell everyone what we had got up to in the hut I told him they would not believe him he then told me that he would get Kim to verify it all happened as she would do any thing for him I did not want this to come out and I knew what he was saying was true so once again I went back to him and his promises because how could I hold my head up and look my work colleagues in the face if he told them about the three of us Kim Peter and myself.

We were together a few months in a flat he rented in the town when he started to lift his hand to me again I suffered beating after beating for about a year when one day I could not take any more I was screaming at him to leave me alone when all of a sudden I found an open razor in my hand and I told him to leave me alone or else I would use it on him as it was either him or me he then went for me a struggle broke out and he managed to get the razor off me he put the razor to my face and he told me he would slice me up and that I belonged to him and after he was finished with me no one would ever look at me again I was petrified he would do it as his eyes were bulging out of his head he then told me that I had to beg for mercy if I wanted to live I begged him not to cut me with the razor he then told me to say he was the master I was his slave only after I said theses words did he release his hold on me as soon as he let me go I ran to the window and I shouted on some one to help me I got one leg out of the window as I knew what was going to happen to me as we were two flights up I knew that if I jumped I would probably kill myself and if I went back into the room there was just as much chance of Peter killing me I never got the choice of jumping or going back into the room as Peter got hold of me by my clothes and he tried to haul me back into the room I held on to the wall at either end of the window but he was to strong for me he got me back in the window slammed it close and he kicked me all over as I curled myself into a ball he grabbed my hair and he held the razor to my throat I though this it I am going to die I then managed to kick him he let me go and then the razor went flying I fought him I really fought him that night because if I was going to die I would die fighting for my life where I got the strength from I do not know then as we were rolling around the room fighting he suddenly stopped hitting me got up and dragged me up with him and then very calmly he told me I was his wife in the eyes of god and that he will never let me go .

He just turned and walked out of the room leaving me lying there on the bed my head started to hurt and so did my leg I looked at my leg and I noticed that the boot on my right leg was cut I managed to get my boot off and then I noticed that my leg had a cut on it and it was bleeding as it was a straight cut I knew that I must of rolled on to the razor at some point when Peter and I were fighting on the floor and I still have the scar on my leg till this day .

Thing settled down again and after a few weeks Peter went out on the town and as usual I was locked in the house I did not care just as long as he was leaving me alone and I did not have to sit in the same room as him for fear of doing something wrong or saying the wrong thing I watched some television then went to bed praying that Peter would come back in a good mood as I was so tired I just wanted to sleep I did sleep but was woken by Peter telling me to get up I did as he told me he then told me to make him a cup of coffee as I was making the coffee someone knocked on the front door Peter got up and answered it he then came into the room with some one I looked and once again Kim was standing there I asked Peter what was going on he then calmly told me that he was going back to Kim as he had no use for me I had served my purpose and that he did not love me he then went through to the bedroom packed his clothes and then as he was going out the door he told me to come to him as I did what he asked he punched me in the face and just walked out of my life I don't know how long I sat there before I went and cleaned my face as my nose had started to bleed I cleaned myself up and just lay on my bed crying and sobbing my heart out how could he do that to me yet again why chase me all over the place to get me back then go back to Kim I could not understand it I did not want to understand it I could not think any more the next morning I went to the outpatients at the hospital got an my nose x-rayed he had broken my nose so I had to go and get it reset at the hospital a few days later .

I met up with a friend of mine from school and we decided to get a flat together I was working in an office and my friend Shoney was working at nights we had a good time week days we worked and at the weekend we partied this was going on for a few months and we met these two guys pervious that we took them home after we all had a night out I was drunk in fact we were all drunk Shoney took her boyfriend through to her room and took mine through to my room I was that drunk I must of fell asleep right away then I was awoken by some one saying my name I could not get my eyes open I just kept falling asleep again then all of a sudden I was cold I tried to pull the covers over me but could not find them then I suddenly the cold woke me up I did not know where I was when I opened my eyes all I knew I was not in my bed when I fully recovered I was standing outside on the veranda with Peter holding me up I could not believe it I did not want to believe it he then told me he will be back in the morning to see me when he left I ran to wake Shoney up I shouted on her to wake up when she eventually woke up I told her all about Peter she told me I must have been dreaming and how could Peter get into the flat when the door was closed and how did he manage to get me out the bed with my boyfriend lying beside me I did not know I told her all I knew was that he did it .

The next morning Shoney asked me to explain about last night again and I did we could not figure how he got in and we were still trying to figure it out when all of a sudden Peter appeared in the room I hid behind the wall partition he told me to come out from where I was hiding I did as he asked he then told me to make him a cup of tea my friend Shoney told him to make his own he told her to shut up or else she would get a slap that's when Shoney said he would try it and he did he slapped Shoney right across the mouth and then he started to call her a whore I told him to leave off her he then told me to shut up or else I would get a slap to .

That was when the truth about Shoney came out her night job was prostitution I never even knew all I knew she always had money apparently Peter had been watching us both for a long time now and he would follow her at night to see what she was up to I was shocked to say the least but she was my friend and what she did was her business I never condoned her in any way who was I to judge any one after that episode in the hut she had her reason I supposed and it was her life .

Peter then told me that he wanted to talk to me on my own so Shoney left the room and then Peter told me that he wanted me back I thought here we go again I asked him about Kim and once again he told me he left her then he walked across and he kissed me on the mouth he then told he was moving in that night and for me to get rid of Shoney by the time he got back how could I tell my friend to go but I did not have to as Shoney told me she heard every word he said and that not to worry as she always had some where to go so Shoney moved out that night and Peter moved in .

So once again Peter was in my life and we were together about three months when Peter asked me if I would go on the game for him as money was short as Peter made me pack up my day job in the office so we were just living off income support I just looked at him I could not say any thing I was shocked that he could ask me to do this he then said if I loved him I would do it and that as my pimp he would not let anything happen to me I told him I would not do it any thing but that he then told me that my friend did it and he asked me if I was ashamed of my friend I said no he then got up and he told me he was going out and that he would not be long I heard the key going into the lock and I heard the lock click shut .

While Peter was away I had a good think to myself once again I was in his trap and I had no way of getting out of it why do I always let him get away with what he does to me that was easy I still loved him and feared him at the same time Peter was away most of the day when I heard him open the door he came into the room and he threw some bags at me and he told me to have a wash and get dressed with what was in the bags as I looked in the bags there was all this lovely underwear stockings suspenders and a few dresses I asked him if he was taking me out for the night he said yes so I wondered what had brought this on so I got washed dressed and before I knew it we were sitting in a pub in the town and it was mostly women and when I looked up I saw my friend Shoney she just gave me a shrug and motioned for me to go to the toilet I told Peter I was going to the toilet and once I was in there Shoney told me what Peter was up to she told me that he had been in a few times through the week and that he was planning on putting me on the game I told her I did not believe her she then told me he spoke to a few of the other girls and found out where they go for to be picked up after I went back to my table I asked Peter if it was true that he was going to send me out on to the streets to sell my body he said not to listen to Shoney as she was talking nonsense so we stayed in the pub for a few hours then we went home I was so relieved that Peter had decided not to put me on the game .

We were not long home when there was a knock on the door I thought here we go Kim was back on the scene but it was not Kim who came in but some guy Peter took him through to the bedroom and they were talking the next thing I knew Peter told me to get through there and do what I have to do as the guy had already paid him for my body and if I even try to protest he would give me such a beating I would not be able to walk for a week so I did not retaliate I got up and walked through to the bedroom and I let this guy abuse me as he had paid for my body after he had finished I just lay there on the bed when the next thing I knew Peter came in took his clothes off and then he started to have sex with me there and then I did not care as this was the start of my long road to prostitution as Peter had all these guys coming to the flat and he would be paid well in advance not that I seen any thing off the money because I didn't all I got was new clothes and underwear and a few digs in the ribs when it suited him he would never mark my face no that never got touched he made sure of that .

As I was sitting in my bed one day Peter came in and he started to drill a hole in the wall I asked him what he was doing he told me he was putting a hole in so that he can watch me with the men and if I ever looked like I was enjoying it he would give me a beating so while these men were having sex with me he was looking through this hole in the wall and when the men left he would asked me if I enjoyed having sex I would say no then he would hit me and tell me I was lying and then he would have sex with me .

STRENGTH FROM WITHIN

The more these men abused me the more I hated myself as far as I was concerned it was not me they were having sex with but someone else it was the only way I coped with the situation my life was taking a downward spiral I felt nothing for me or the life I was leading because every emotion I had in my body had frozen I didn't care any more what happened to me I had past caring then one night Peter took me down town to pick up more customers he told me that I could work the streets as well as from the flat I was in and out of cars all night handing Peter money every time I came back with a punter my life carried on like this for about eight months until one night I went away with a punter in a car he took me to a secluded spot he told me to get out of the car I did as he asked then he told me to lie on the grass and not to move he then ripped my top off me I asked him what he was going to do he told me to shut up and not move some instinct told me to lie very still I lay there in the middle of nowhere in the pitch black while this guy did all these kind of things to me after he finished he told me to get up I did as he told me then we got back inside his car I never said anything to him it was when we were back into the town I asked him for my money he told me that he does not pay scum like me and then he took my bag and then he told me to get out I could not get out of that car fast enough I walked to where I knew Peter would be waiting and I told him what happened he then got angry and he hit me in the ribs and he told me that I was a stupid bitch because I did not have any money to give him he then took me home and once we were there he hit me again I told him this was the end I had took enough of the abuse from him and the men I had to sleep with for money he told me that I will keep doing it until he says I can stop so I pleaded with him to let me stop as I told him I could have been killed by that guy he said mores the pity he then told me to get washed and get into bed as he wanted to know all that this guy did to me so I had to go through every detail with him and then Peter told me to have sex with him after he had finished I lay there in the dark and I decided I was going to kill myself as this was the only way I could escape this life and Peter so once I knew that Peter was sleeping I crept out of bed as not to waken him and I went to the bathroom and then took the blade out of his razor and I slit one of my wrists and then I was just away to do the other when Peter came in and caught me he took the blade out of my hand as I told him I just wanted to die as I could not live this life any more and then I started to cry he then led me to me out of the bathroom and he cleaned my wrist and was busy wrapping my wrist with a bandage when he told me I was a fool as slitting my wrist would not accomplish any thing I told him it would give me peace as that was all I wanted was peace and out of this world he then led me to my bed and he made me drink a cup of tea and he gave me two tablets and he told me to swallow them I took them and the next thing I knew it was morning.

When I woke up Peter came into the room carrying a tray with some breakfast on it I told him I was not hungry he told me to eat it I tried my best to eat what was in front of me but I felt so sick I just wanted to go to sleep and never ever wake up I asked Peter to please leave me alone he then told me that he would never leave me alone and that he would make me well again I did not want him to make me well again I didn't want to see him or anything else again I wanted out of this world permanently .

For a whole week I stayed in the flat while Peter ran around doing this and that but I was mostly asleep as Peter kept giving me these pills and they knocked me out I did not care I was happy as I did not have to think or do any thing any more until Peter came in one day he told me that he was going to take me back to the Downs I told him I did not want to go back there he told me it would be different there and that he was just thinking about me and my health and that what I needed was peace and quiet so once again like a dog to the slaughter I was on the bus to the Downs we where there for a month when Peter mentioned how would I feel if I went back to prostitution I told him no way he then told me that he could bring the clients to me as he had the chance of a car I just looked at him that's when I realized he did not give a dam about me he was more interested in the money so once again I had to think about what I was going to do so after along debate with him I decided to tell Peter that I would do it but I needed some water to have a bath he said good girl he picked up the water container and when he stepped out the door I gave him a couple of minutes then I got a knife and I ran out of the door and I ran to the far end of the field as fast as I could and I managed to get one of the hut door open with the knife that I had taken with me as I had seen Peter do it often enough when we ran out of food as I closed the door I heard him shouting on me and what he will do to when he gets hold of me I was shaking with fear I could not breath I was gasping for air but I knew I had to stay where I was for my own safety .

As it was so dark in the hut I searched around with my hands till I found a bed and I lay down on it my heart was racing I heard Peter trying the doors of the huts I prayed to god that he did not try this one I don't know how long I stayed in that hut but it must have been hours as I could not come out before it was dark as I could not risk getting caught so I went to the door and I slowly opened it and listening for any noise I crept out of there I was slowly making my way in between the huts to get to the road so that I could try and hitch a lift back to Dundee I was just about out of the field when I was grabbed from behind I screamed as loud as I could but there was no one to hear my screams but the darkness as the place was deserted Peter dragged me back to the hut and he hit me over and over again he then told me that as I kept running away he would make sure I never would never escape from him again he got a chain and padlock and he wrapped the chain around my ankle and then he put the chain around the metal bars of the bed and he left me like that I could not move any further than a few feet then at times he would chain me by my wrists for a whole week on and off I was chained to that bed until he told me that we were going back to Dundee as he had business to attend to and that he had to sign on at the labour exchange and he warned me not to even think about running away as I knew better than to try it so we arrived at Dundee and at the labour exchange while Peter was signing on these two men came a told him he was under arrest I just looked at Peter and he asked them what he was getting arrested for they told him he would find out once they got him to the police station as they matched Peter out of the door I got hold of one of the officers and I asked him how long Peter would be away for he told me that he had a few outstanding fines and they wanted to see him about another matter as I walked over to the car Peter shouted at me to go and see his mother for the money for the fines I told him I would go but as soon as the car drove off I had no intentions of going to see his mother so I turned and walked away not knowing where I was going or what I was going to do but as usual I ended up at my friend Carols house as she was my saviour in those days she never ever refused me any kind of shelter she was like a big sister to me and for that I will always thank her.

I read in the papers that Peter had got six months for theft and none payments of fines so I was free of him for at least six months and as far as I was concerned I would be free of him for good as a few days later I was sitting in a lawyers office applying for a divorce and I sent him a nice letter to the jail explaining all this.

STRENGTH FROM WITHIN

SAMUEL AND LILY

I had been going out with this guy for a few months his name was Robert when I found out I was pregnant and when I told Robert I was pregnant he told me he was happy but he had a worried look on his face I asked him what was wrong he then told me that he had something to tell me I asked him what it was he then he told me that he was married to some one I just looked at him I could not believe what I was hearing I told him to get out of my flat to say I was hurt and angry would be an under statement I was devastated once again I found myself in a right mess pregnant and alone I could not stay in my flat so I went to stay with my friend Colleen I had known Colleen since I was sixteen I told her all about Robert and how he was married so once again I just got on with my life I stayed with Colleen on and off all through my pregnancy and in between Robert would keep coming to my flat or to my friend Colleens house also his wife had came to my flat a few times with one of her friends as Robert had told me a few times that he was away from his wife Gillian as I knew he would never leave his wife so I told him I wanted nothing more to do with him he would not leave me alone so I had decided I had to go and fix things once and for all I went to Roberts house with a few of his belongings my friend Colleen came with me when we arrived at Roberts house I knocked on his door and his wife answered I explained that Robert would not leave me alone and that I wanted nothing more to do with him she told us both to come in as we all sat talking she told me she knew Robert went with other women but as long as he always came back to her she let him do his own thing I told her I was so sorry for ever getting involved with her husband I just got the words out of my mouth when we heard the door opening as I turned around I saw Robert standing there he told my friend and I to get out of his house after hearing this I knew exactly where I stood with him so I just walked out I told him that as I had brought all his belongings with me then there was no reason for him to come back into my life .

Colleen and I were not long back in her house when there was a knock at her door Colleen went to answer it she was not long gone when she came and told me that Robert was at her door wanting to see me I could not believe it so I went to the door and told him I wanted nothing more to do with him and that he had a hard neck coming here as he had not that long ago he had threw me out of his house he told me he did not know what else to do as he was shocked to see me and Colleen sitting there in his house I told him I had enough and that all the stress was making me ill and that I had to think about the baby I then closed the door in his face.

As I was in regular contact with my family I was staying with them for the new year it was 1977 and my baby was due very soon I went into labour on the fourth of January in my parents house I had a really bad time having my baby as I was in labour for forty eight hours and then I had to have a section as the baby was stuck he was to big for me to have a normal delivery.

My son Samuel was born on the sixth of January 1977 I was twenty five he was a lovely baby I remember looking down at him in his cot in the hospital and thinking here is someone whom I love with all my heart and he was all mine I could not believe I had a son I used to keep hold of his cot all the time I would even fall asleep like this it was as if I was afraid someone would steal him away from me when I was sleeping.

I took my son home a week later and we were getting along just fine just the two of us things could not of been any better when one day there was a knock on my door I just sat there holding my baby as I knew if it had been my family they would of shouted through the letter box so I kept very quiet then I heard Samuels father shouting through the letter box I went to the door and asked him what it was he wanted he told me that he wanted to see his son as I did not put Samuels dads name on my sons birth certificate he had no claim to him he then pleaded with me to let him see his son so I relented and let him in as he held his son he told me that he was leaving his wife for me and Samuel I told him I did not want him to leave his wife so he accepted my decision but we did become good friends as he told me Gillian had no problems regarding him coming to see his son so when ever I wanted to go out any where Robert would baby sit Samuel for me I was out one night and as I came back I heard a females voice coming from the living room as I walked in I heard her tell Robert that he should take his son home with him as I walked into the living room I saw that Robert was with his wife Gillian I told the two of them to get out as no one was taking my son away and I told her that as Robert was not on Samuels birth certificate there was nothing he could do and that he had no right to try and take Samuel away from me and I told her that they would have a fight on there hands me she told me that as Samuels father he did have rights I never saw Robert for a long time after that episode .

Samuel was just 10months old when I met this guy he was called Alan Vale and yes he was married to Kim we both met up at the divorce court about a year ago when we were both granted a divorce .

Alan asked me out on one occasion I said no to the fact he used to be married to Kim at one point in his life and a few months later I bumped into him again and again he asked me to go out with him when I thought why not so after a few months I moved in with Alan with my son Samuel we were getting along fine when one day there was a knock on the door and Alan went to answer it the next thing I knew there was a lot of shouting I went to see what was going on when I saw the pair of them standing there Peter and Kim I asked what the hell was going on Kim started to shout at me that I was not bringing her kids up as Alan was awarded the full custody of there two children a boy and a girl I told her that it had nothing to do with her or Peter what we did as we were all divorced from each another as I was talking to Kim I could feel Peters eyes on me and when I looked he just gave this look as if to say what the hell are you doing eventually after about twenty minutes they left as Alan was not taking any crap from them or I for that matter my main concern was my son and his children as there were all in the house at the time .

We never saw them again after that so Alan and I were living a nice life with the children when I found out I was pregnant again so we both decided to get married by this time I was four months pregnant we were married in the local register office my married life with Alan lasted exactly six weeks as one night we had a quarrel and he went to lift his hands to me so I quickly got up and picked up a little baby chair and hit him with it then I calmly picked up Samuel and walked out of his life I had enough beating from Peter in the past there was no way I was going to let any man hit me again .

So once again I found myself at my parents house with Samuel as I was five and a half months pregnant I went to my doctor to see about an abortion as I did not think I could manage on my own with two little children so I was booked in a few weeks later for the abortion I never kept that appointment I had decided to go it alone once more so my daughter Lily was born three months premature weighing exactly three and a half pounds she was born on the 14[th]Febuary 1978 as she was so small she was in the special baby unit in the hospital for about a month before I got her home I notified her father he came to see her once with me at the hospital then I never saw him again he was not interested in his daughter.

By the time I got Lily home I had my own little flat just for the three of us Samuel Lily and myself I was doing fine with the kids but Lily would cry and cry most nights I was up every night with Lily and sometimes I would not get much sleep then I had to be up for Samuel as Samuel was not keeping to good he had the illness a stomach bug the doctor told me that he would put Samuel into the hospital for sick kids as he did not want Lily to catch it as she was still a small baby I phoned my mother and I told her what the doctor said about Samuel having to go into hospital she then started to shout at me over the phone about how I did not care about Samuel and all I cared about was Lily I told her this was not true she then informed me that she had no interest in Lily what so ever and that she did not care about her all she cared about was Samuel I was totally shocked at her reaction and told her it was not true and that I loved them both the same I had to put the phone down as I was so upset how could she say that about her own grand daughter and say that about how I had no time for Samuel every time I argued with my mother she always managed to make me feel bad inside and then I would go on these guilt trips.

Samuel came home after a week in the hospital then one night I had to get the doctor to come and see Lilly as she was having a lot of problems with her breathing she seemed to be fighting to get a breath the doctor came out and told me that Lily had a very bad cold but she would be fine I had a bad night with her that night I sat up with her so the next day I was so tired I had to drag myself out of bed and feed Samuel and see to Lily as Lily was still having problems I phoned the doctor again and I was told she will be fine so that night I put them both to bed and once again I had problems with Lily I eventually got her back to sleep and I went through into the living room I sat on the couch and I fell asleep I woke up thinking I could hear Lily but no there was nothing I woke up in the morning with Samuel crying very loudly I ran into the bedroom picked him up gave him a cuddle then took him through to the living room then I went back into the bedroom and to check on Lily I picked her up and as her eyes were open I said hello then I realized she was not moving my darling daughter was dead I just put her down into the pram and all I remember was that I banged on a neighbours door and the next thing my house was full of police and ambulance men and friends of the family as they had come to take the kids picture I was in shock as the next thing I can remember was I was at my parents house and I was sitting in there living room and my parents and family friends were all talking I could not hear them properly as everything was all muffled it was as if someone had covered my ears with something I guess I was in shock my days were so unreal and my nights were my nightmare because as soon as I closed my eyes I would hear this baby cry things got so bad for me the doctor gave my mother pills for me take I did not feel much at this time in my life all I did know was that my darling precious daughter was dead the funeral came and went and I did not feel anything at all I was numb I was still living with my parents when one morning about one or two in the morning I was sitting in the living room when I heard my parents come in my parents sat down in there separate chairs and as soon as my mother sat down she started to shout at me accusing me of killing her grand daughter Lily before I could say anything my father got up from his chair and he slapped my mother across the face telling her to shut up as it was not true I looked at my mother with contempt and I just walked out of my parents house and went back to my flat I left Samuel with my parents until I could get someone to go and collect him as I had made up my mind I would never go back to my parents house ever again .

When I got to my flat I made myself a drink of tea and I sat and I swallowed a few of the pills the doctor had given my mother I had no desire to live I didn't care any more my parents would look after Samuel I just wanted out and away from the pain I was suffering I lay down on the bed waiting to die when the next thing I knew someone was shouting my name and shaking me I eventually came to and I saw my brother Mark he asked me if I was feeling all right I told him what I done and why he then told me that he heard what my mother had said to me and that was the reason he came to my flat to make sure I was fine as he had a feeling I was going to swallow some pills he told me he knocked a few times on the door and when he never got an answer he kicked my door in Mark made me get up and we talked about my relationship with my mother he told me he knew my mother did not like me as she told him I never mention the sexual abuse by my father as I knew he would blame me Mark told me that I had Samuel took look after now and that I should not listen to my mother regarding my daughters death but for me it was to late the words had been spoken the following night Mark brought Samuel back to me and once again I tried to get on with my life even though I had this big hole inside of me I felt as if part of me was missing .

About a month after Lily died I was told Lily died of a cot death the day she died was exactly three months to the date that she was born as she died on the 14th May 1978.

STRENGTH FROM WITHIN

MY BREAKDOWN

I met my husband Gordon a few months after the death of Lily and a year later I had another daughter we named her Abigail after me as we had decided if it was a boy we would call him after his father and if it was a girl we would call her after me Abigail was born 19th May 1979 my daughter was not long born when I started to get these nightmare over and over again the nightmare consisted of me walking into a room dressed just in my nightdress and as I looked around the room all the walls were covered with black velvet and in the middle of the room there was a table and sitting on the table was a little white coffin and I walked towards the coffin and I looked into it but I could not see who was in it and then at this point I always woke up I had this nightmare a few weeks when I went to the doctor and he gave me sleeping pills and he also suggested that I should go and see some one about the nightmares I told him I would be fine .

Abigail was a month old and I was feeding her when she started to choke I more or less threw her at her father and I ran out of the house I panicked I ran to the neighbour and I asked her to please phone an ambulance while we were waiting on the ambulance I was pacing my bedroom and praying to god to not let my baby die

Gordon shouted on me to come through to the living room I told him I couldn't he then told me Abigail was fine as I went into the living room Gordon had Abigail lying on her belly across his knees and he was rubbing her back he gave her to me and I was holding her when the ambulance arrived we were driven to the hospital and when we arrived there my gynaecologist was standing in the reception area with some other doctors he told me that they were there to take Abigail away to make sure she was fine I just kept hold of her I was afraid to let her go in case I never saw her again my gynaecologist managed to talk me round to handing her over after Abigail was checked over they told me she was fine and that all that happened was that her milk went down the wrong way and even though this looked frightening to watch she was fine they kept Abigail in the hospital for a week they told me it was just to give me peace of mind and they were right .

After the week was over we brought Abigail home from the hospital that's when I started to kick her carrycot to make sure she would move before I would pick her up then I would call her Lily at times my life carried on like this for about five months when I started to have problems with Samuel as he would hit his sister I tried to get him to leave her alone I had to watch him like a hawk in case he hurt her bad Samuels behaviour got that bad that every time Samuel hit Abigail I hit him then I would sit and cry and feel guilty I hit him until one day I realized I was doing what my mother did to me all those years ago so I decided there and then that I was not going to bring my son up the way my mother brought me up so I phoned his real father and I asked him if he would come over so that I could talk to him Robert came over and I told him what was happening he agreed to take Samuel for a month to give me a break so he told me to have Samuel ready that night about tea time so I packed his little suitcase and I tried to explain to Samuel the best I could what was going to happen he just nodded his head as we sat and waited on Robert coming for his son my head was going round in circles I just wanted to run away to escape as the time came and went for Robert to come for his son I realized that he was not coming so I unpacked Samuels suitcase and told him he was not going away after all so I tried my best to keep everything together and to keep sane at the same time until one day Samuel hit Abigail with a metal shovel I was out at the time and Gordon told me that while he was doing something in the house he heard Abigail crying he went through to the room and there was Samuel with the shovel in his hand I took hold of my son and I hit him I then told Gordon I was going to see my parents to see if they would take Samuel for me as I really could not deal with this any more as I had not seen my parents for a few months as I was dreading going to see them but I had no other choice .

As I knocked on my parents door my heart was in

my mouth for some reason I waited till my brother Mark opened the door I asked him if both my parents were in he said yes I walked into the living room and just as I sat down I started to cry I then told my parents about the problems I was having with Samuel and I asked them if they could take there grandson just to give a break I was waiting on there answer when my mother told me that no they were not taking Samuel as he was my son and that it was up to me to look after him then she started to tell me I had a son as well as a daughter I just turned and left there house and went back home when I got in Gordon asked me what they said I told him what my mother said he just said typical as he knew my mother never really took to Abigail I told him she never took to Lily either I just tried to get on with my life the best I could until one day I sat Abigail on the floor with her toys she was about seven months old and as Samuel was in the living room to I told him to behave and to leave Abigail alone they were both playing away everything was fine I had to go to the toilet as I was washing my hands I heard Abigail scream I ran through to the living room and there she was lying back on the floor as we had stone floors in the houses I was so frightened that she had hurt her head I got hold of Samuel and I asked him if he had pushed Abigail he just nodded his head saying yes I phoned my health visitor and explained what happened she came out with my doctor who examined Abigail then he told me that he was worried about me as it looked as if I would need eyes in the back off my head to keep everything under control as to Samuel hitting Abigail he told me that I needed help and that he would recommend for Samuel to go and see a child doctor to see why he was hitting his sister .

A month and a half later I got a letter from the hospital to take Samuel to see a specialist as I was sitting in his room he asked me all about the problems I was having with Samuel I told him he then told me to go and wait outside while he spoke to Samuel I sat outside in the waiting room for about twenty minutes when I was told to go back into the room as I sat down the specialist told me that Samuel was a bright boy and that he knew what he was doing when he was hitting Abigail and that he was not neglected in any way I was then told to come back with him at a later date in between the time I had to go back to see the specialist Samuel kept hitting Abigail and I would smack him .

The next visit to the specialist came round and he asked how things were going and I told him more or less just the same he then told me to go out into the waiting room again after about twenty minute I had to go back in and see him and this time a nurse took Samuel out to the play area and then once we were on our own the specialist told me that as he said before Samuel was clever and that as he knew what he was doing there was a chance that either Samuel would really hurt Abigail or there was a chance that I would hurt him and with all the stress I was living with there was a good chance I would kill myself he then floored me with his next suggestion he told me that he was advising me to put my son up for adoption as things were never going to get any better I stood up and I told him I came for some help regarding my son not to be told to adopt him out I took my son home and I told Gordon what the specialist said regarding putting my son up for adoption he told me that things would not get that bad so again we all pulled together and just tried to deal with the situation the best we could .

Things carried on as usual until I could not take any more I was crying not eating going about like a zombie with the pills I was giving from the doctor again Samuel hurt Abigail I had no one to turn to no one to take my son so I had no option but to phone social services I told then I had hit my son and that I could not cope so a social worker came out to see me and I told her what had been going on over there the past two years she took my son away he was fostered out to give me a break and I would go and see him I hated seeing him with his foster parents but here was nothing I could do as I was so ill at the time in my life even though I did not know it the social services asked me to adopt my son out I said no and I went to the school he was attending and I took my son out of school I then took him back home with me we were in the living room when the front door went and as I opened the door the social worker asked me if I had my son I said yes she then told me I had no right to do that and that if I ever try it again they would get the police involved she then told me I had lost my rights as a mother so I had to watch will they walked out of my house with my son I just sat and cried and cried then I walked up to his picture on the wall took it down and I never looked at it again .

After what happened to Samuel I told Gordon I wanted another child so I went and got the coil out and we tried for another baby I fell pregnant after a few moths and I was three months pregnant when I was sitting in the house when I got an awful pain in my stomach I went to the toilet and I could see I was bleeding down below I went to see my next door neighbour as Gordon was not in she phoned for an ambulance I was taken to the hospital where I lost my baby by this time Gordon came to the hospital I was devastated to say the least my life took a down ward tumble after loosing my baby I had lost the will to live I was under five stone had these terrible thoughts I could not go any where unless Gordon was with me I felt as if I was being smothered and I was fighting for a breath I would think there was no air outside I was afraid of water you name it I was afraid of it and I just could not cope I was so afraid of life itself I tried to kill myself with all my pills I was taken into the hospital and I was released after they pumped my stomach and it was only after I saw a doctor at a hospital for the mentally ill that they put me into hospital for my own good I did not know what time of day it was or what I was doing I was so preoccupied by what was going on in my head everything was going past me the doctors at the hospital told me that there would be a psychologist coming to see me the next day as I lay in my bed that night and all these horrors going on in my head I looked out and up to the sky I saw this white shape in the sky then it changed into a brilliant white angel I just lay there looking at it and then it disappeared slowly as if it was melting away.

I must of fell asleep after that just looking up at the dark night sky I woke up and I looked up at the sky hoping to see my angel but there was nothing just the blue sky I did not want to be there I wanted this angel to take me away with her to release me from this prison I was in within myself .

A nurse came over to my bed and she took me to meet this psychologist her name was Tyler she told me to sit down and as I just sat there looking at she asked me a few questions then the next thing I knew all my past came rushing out of my mouth it was as if I had no control of what I was saying even the sexual abuse from my father came out and then I was crying she asked me to try and explain what was going on inside of me my emotions and feelings I told her about the horrors in my head I told her it was like as if I was living and walking in a nightmare and I could not get out of it she told me that she would get me better but first I had to come off the pills the doctor prescribed to me as they were not doing me no good so she told me that I will get no more pills and that she would see me every day to help me through the with drawl symptoms .

So I was taken off the pills at once and after a few days I started to get the sweats shaking and the sickness all at once I felt so bad and every day I saw Tyler I told her what I was experiencing and how I was feeling she helped me by telling me what these feelings were and how long they would last I remember sitting there on my bed and watching these things go up the wall I was not afraid I just watched them on the wall after a while I lay down on my bed and when I looked back at the wall they were gone and I told Tyler about these things on the wall and she told me I was hallucinating as Tyler took me through everything I came to the conclusion that if any thing bothered or frightened me I would say to myself Tyler will explain it all she will help you and that's what got me through the bad days every session I had with Tyler I would ask her how long will it be before I am better she would just say to me take a day at a time and I had too as I was getting the bad palpitations my heart was beating so fast every day I was sweating and I was frightened I was never so frightened as what I was when the palpitations stopped I thought I had died as my body was so quiet I did not hear this noise in my head it was too quiet I panicked a nurse must of seen that I was agitated she asked me if I was all right I told her what was happening she told me not to be frightened as my body was just getting back to normal from all the drugs I was taken I was getting rid of the side affects a few nights after that I took a bad turn I had this feeling inside of me to scream so I screamed and screamed I just kept saying I wanted out Tyler explained to me that what I was really saying was the real me was trying to get out as I had kept myself in check for all those years my feelings were coming to the surface I told her I did not like feeling like this she told me that I should be feeling this way as she would be worried about me if I didn't go through any emotional feelings she then told me that I was on the road to recovery she told me that she thought it was a good idea if I went home I panicked at the thought of going home and I told her she told me she will still come and see me every day until I am past the worse so I went home to Gordon and Abigail it was coming up for Christmas and they had the tree up and the decorations on the walls it looked nice but still I was getting the cramps in my stomach but I was starting to eat I only ate a small amount at first I was still four and a half stone .

My first session with Tyler when I got home was about my father I told her about how he sexually abused me when I was a small girl and how my mother blamed me for the abuse she told me that as I was a very small child it was not my fault but my parents fault as they were the adults and I was the child and that my mother knew what was going on long before I came to realize what he was doing was bad that's when she told me my mother allowed it to happen and as she must have been afraid of my father to question him so ease her own guilt she put her guilt on to me and that's why I carried the guilt inside off me for all those years she then told me that I must tell the rest of the family about my fathers abuse I told her that I never even told Gordon my husband about the abuse she told me to start there tell Gordon I told her I couldn't as he would leave me she told me he will not leave me and to trust her so I told Gordon after I picked up the courage to tell him he was shocked to say the least he started to call my father all the perverts under the sun and no he never left me .

My next port of call was the family my sister came up to see me and I told her what dad had done to me and she told me that he tried to do the same to her but never told any one so I told her I was going to tell the rest of the family as I had taken the blame of it for to long and it just about destroyed me so I next told my brother Marks wife Helen she then told the rest of the family and they in turn went against me telling me I was a born liar so they all alienated me which did not bother me in the least as I never saw any of them any way my mother made a good job of turning my family against me .

That's when the silent phone calls started they would call all hours of the day and night so I had to deal with all this as well as what was going on in my head .

I was home about a month when one day I just out my bed when I had this sick feeling I told Tyler about it she told me to go to the doctor which I did do and I was told I was pregnant and that the doctor advised me to get rid of the baby I looked at him and I told him I lost my daughter to a cot death and I miscarriage another one and he can sit there and tell me I must terminate this pregnancy I got up to leave he then told me that he wanted to see my husband Gordon so a few days later we went back to see the doctor the doctor told Gordon what he told me he explained that as I was still under five stone I would never ever carry the baby full time and to loose another child would put me right back to where I was when I was in the mental hospital so Gordon told me that he would rather have me better than have another baby and to think about the consequences so after a lot of soul searching I went ahead with the abortion and had a sterilization at the same time as I could not go through all that again after a few days of coming home from the hospital I went through this very bad guilt trip of what I just did to my baby Tyler explained to me this was normal and that I would get through it I was getting panic attacks all the time she told me they will settle down I thought I was going off my head again she also told me I had to do it to for my own health and that it was through medical reasons it happened nothing else and not to hate myself but no matter what she said to me I was going through these horrendous thoughts and feeling after a few days after the abortion I would sit and cry I felt so suicidal and I told Tyler this she told me that the feelings would go it was terrible having to deal with these thought of suicide I had to fight my thoughts to stay sane I prayed to god every day to give me the strength to cope and to fight for my sanity and life.

After a few weeks Tyler got me to talk about was Lily and her death I told her I could not do that as it was to painful for me to talk about she then told me I must talk about it so that I can move on with my life I told her I had moved on she said I never got over her death because my mother blamed me and I took the blame that night my mother told me I killed her and that I had been living for my daughter that died I asked how that could be possible as I knew she was dead she told me I knew but I would not accept it so I had to go through every thing with Tyler from the day I had her to the day she died she also told me that a lot of my guilt came from the fact I was going to go for an abortion when I was five months pregnant so after I spoke about Lily I went through the grieving period as Lily had been dead five years by this time but to me it was as if she had just died it was as if it just happened that day .

This was a terrible time in my life as I had to talk about the past and with it came the

panic attacks the suicidal thoughts and the bad feelings I was on one long roller coaster ride but I knew myself that I had to do it to get better but what really got me through the really bad times was talking to god and asking for him to give me the strength to carry on when I felt myself weaken and I did weaken on and off I had good days I had bad days I still could not go any where on my own I was a prisoner in my own home but I was still seeing Tyler and she would take me out in her car I felt safe with her but no one else as I was still talking about Lily I was told that it would be an good idea to go and visit her grave I told Tyler I don't want to go so as usual Tyler talked me into going with her a few days later as we were driving through the cemetery gates I felt like running away and I told Tyler what I was feeling at that time she told me this was all natural feelings so she asked me where Lily was buried I took her to the spot where I thought was the grave as soon as we stepped out of the car I could not see anything clearly I was looking through a mist and as Tyler asked me what I was feeling I told her that all I can see was a mist she told me there was no mist it was just me and my mind and things will be fine we found the grave I did not know what I felt on that day all I knew was that it all felt so unreal Tyler told me this was normal I hated those feelings we eventually found her grave I just broke down and cried we did not stay long I just wanted away and back home again I made a few trips to the grave with Tyler and I was getting better each time but at the same time I was frightened I was not afraid of the cemetery it was mostly a fear from within .

After Tyler left I had years of counselling from various psychologists and they all told me the same I had numeral issues in my life I still had to deal with it I could not get away from the past as it always came back to haunt me one way or another and when this happened I spoke to god I asked him to give me the strength to fight what ever it was that was bothering me at that time as I lived with some sort of fear every day of my life maybe my parents and Peter tried to destroy me as a person but there is one thing they could never do and that was to destroy my soul as the little flicker of light that was within me grew brighter with each new day that dawned as the years came and went so did my depression as far as I was concerned I was alone even though I had Gordon and Abigail I was stuck in this hell and the only way I could get out was through my faith in god as he gave me the strength to carry on no matter what I was feeling inside I would just sit and cry and then carry on with my life the best I could even though I got so dependent on Gordon I could not go any where unless he was with me and I used to keep Abigail off school so that I would not be on my own it was terrible being afraid all the time my life carried on like this for years until I was put into a group for abused women and it was through this group that I started to realize a lot of my problems were due to my parents as I still was carrying the guilt from the abuse my parents put me through and it was the talking and listening to these other women that I came to realize just where all my fears came from my fear of water came from when my mother tried to drown me in the bath when I was young then I came to realized that every time my mother left me with my father she knew he was abusing me I thought how could she do that to me how could any women do that to there own child or any child for that matter and as for my father well he like my mother let me take the blame they were both more than happy for me to take the blame they did not give a dam about me as a person or as there daughter as when I told the rest of the family about the abuse when I got out of the hospital they both told the same story that as I had been in a mental hospital I did not know what I was saying I got really angry as these weekly session there was a lot of anger inside of me until one day I finally decided I was not taking the blame any more I phoned the police and I told them what my father and mother did to me all those years ago I told the police women everything she then went to see them but they told me that my parents would not answer the door they even went to see my sister she in turn phoned my parents by this time I was obsessed with getting them back I wanted to hurt them they way they hurt me all those years ago and how they turned my own brothers and sister against me I carried this hatred for my parents around with me for years and I would visualise what I would do to my mother if I ever came across her on her own I could of killed her and thought nothing of it then one day it came to me that she was not worth doing the time in jail for as in a way I was still letting her rule my life and only I could stop it as she had put me into my own prison cell from when I was an abused child I was locked into this prison but there was no warden to turn the key to let me out only I could do that I had free myself from the physiological chains that were binding me and hold my head up high as I had nothing to be ashamed of this was not an easy thing to do as I had lived with the guilt for so long I had to learn to love myself and every day I told myself in front of a mirror that I was a nice person and not the bad person my parents had me believing for years.

It was while I was attending the abused group that a visitor came to my door when I was out and told my daughter Abigail that my father was seriously ill in hospital I phoned all the hospitals to see where he was and what was wrong but not one of them knew about him so a friend of mine went to see one of my cousins and my cousin came to see me she told me my father had died two days previous I was shocked to say the least not one of the family told me he had died as a few days previous I had heard my fathers brother had died and I dreamt that me father had died just a few days later and I told Gordon about this dream that I had and I told him I was getting my father mixed up with my uncle.

I was so confused about my feelings for my father as I cried and cried and I could not understand how I was feeling like this after what he done to me I had to phone the day hospital to talk to my counsellor as I was in an awful state when I went to see her I asked her why I was feeling this way about my father I was torn inside between hating him and hurting because he was dead and part of me hated me for feeling the pain of his death I was fighting a battle with myself she then explained that no matter what he did he was still my father and it was normal to feel sad as he was part of me and me of him it took me a long time to come to terms with these facts and the pain I was feeling my father died on the 14th October 1999 and it was on the boxing day of that year that I saw my big brother at the shops and he then asked me how I was and I asked him why he never told me about my father death he told me that our mother told the family that I wanted nothing to do with any of them I told him this was not true he then invited me to his house the next night so I went along and I spoke to him about my father he told me my father died of a cancerous brain tumour I asked him what time he died at and the time that he mention was exactly the time I dreamt that my father had died my father had came to me in my dream to let me know he was dead as he knew no one in the family had the decency to tell me he had died .

THE CANCER

———————————

I was at the bingo one day when I just about fainted I felt terrible so the next day I went to the doctor she took some blood from me as the blood test came back alright I thought nothing more of the near fainting spell .

One night while after I had a bath my grandson asked to see my boobies as he called my breasts I said no and I leaned down to talk to him and he then nipped my left breast I stepped back with the pain and for a few days the pain came and went as I lay in my bed I felt my left breast and I felt a hard lump I then went back to the doctor she then referred me to have check up at the breast clinic when I received my date to attend the hospital it was the 4th December 2000 my key worker Jill took me I did not worry unduly as I had already had a few checkups on my breasts over the years and they were fine as Jill and I sat in the waiting room I was asked to go for an x-ray on both my breasts after this was done I was told to sit in the waiting room until I was called by the breast nurse when my turn came I went into a room with Jill I was told to lie on this bed and the doctor done a biopsy on my left breast he then told me to go and have a cup of tea for twenty minutes while he got the results back so Jill and I sat in the hospital café and twenty minutes later we were back in the waiting room after a few minutes I was called back into the doctors room I was told to sit down and as I sat down he explained to me that he had found irregular cells in my left breast I then asked him if it was cancer he said yes I just sat there and cried he then told me that I would have to come back in a few days as he had to do another biopsy I walked out that hospital with Jill in shock I could not believe after all I had been through in my life I now had cancer I asked Jill how was I going to tell my daughter I had cancer and most of all how was I going to tell Gordon before I knew it I was outside my daughters house and Jill came in with me she sat there while I had to explain to Abigail that I had cancer as we were talking my friend Colleen came to my daughters door and like me she could not believe that I had cancer as I sat there I could feel all eyes on me I looked at them all and told them I would be fine even though I did not feel fine I don't know what I felt I was in shock .

I got through that day in a daze my friend Colleen stayed with me most of the day then Gordon came home he never said much I was more preoccupied by all the thoughts running through my head I was trying not to panic one minute I would feel this panic rising up inside of me the next I would feel nothing it was awful I phoned Colleen about three in the morning I just could get my head around the fact I had cancer I asked her on the phone why me I told her I did not deserve this .

A few days later saw me back at the hospital with Jill the doctor froze my left breast then he did a big biopsy he then told me that as to where my lump was that he would have to remove my left breast I just sat there as he told me the date of my operation it was to be on the 9th January 2001 I thought what a way to start the new year and the days waiting for my operation was just horrendous I just wanted to take a knife and cut this cancer from me I had to come to terms about the cancer and the fact I had to loose my left breast also I had to come to terms with death as far as I was concerned if you had cancer then you die that was the way of it as far I was concerned .

How I got through the days until my operation was too draw angels and trace holy pictures every thing about god was traced I felt near to god doing this and it helped me a lot it helped me to stay sane as Gordon would not talk to me about the cancer it was as if we did not communicate any longer he would just sit and look at me until one day I just cracked up and shouted at him I told him he could not handle the fact I had cancer and he told me this was true he told me any one else but me after what I had been through in my life and then he started to cry I went over to him and I told him I was not going any where I cuddled him even though it should have been the other way round but that was just the way it was I just had to be strong for both of us .

STRENGTH FROM WITHIN

The day of my operation had come my friend Colleen and Gordon took me to the hospital as we walked through the doors of the hospital I said to Gordon and Colleen I cant believe I am walking through these doors to go and get my breast cut off.

I was taking down to the operation theatre about nine in the morning but what time I came back I don't know all I knew was my friend Colleen was there waiting on me and she stayed with me thought that whole day when it had came to visiting time Gordon and Abigail and her partner came to see me with my grandson it was as if they could not look at me when they were talking to me it was a shock I suppose for them all but I tried to let them know I was fine and feeling fine even though I wasn't I still did not know what I was feeling even though I was sitting there minus one breast

I never slept all that night in the hospital and the next day I asked for a shower so one of the nurses took me to the shower room and with me I took my drains that I had sewn into my body they gave me a little bag to carry them in after my shower I decide to have a look at where my breast used to be as I looked I cried and then after I did my crying I just accepted the fact I had just lost my breast and that I did not miss it as it was cancerous and that was the last time I thought about my breast .

Ruby McKenzie

I had my operation on the Tuesday morning and I was out of the hospital by the Friday night as I was determined to just get on with my life and not let this cancer rule my life so on the 12th January 2001 I walked out of the hospital minus my left breast and short of thirteen lymph glands from my left arm I was told to return the following week for the results regarding my lymph glands that they removed from my left arm so once again a week later saw me and my friend Colleen and myself sitting outside my surgeons office in the hospital as I was called in my friend and I sat down then my surgeon told me that three of my lymph glands had traces of cancer in them and that I had to receive chemotherapy when he told me this I just asked him if I would loose my hair maybe it sound so stupid to some people but that was my main concern at that time in my life as I had long hair and as I had already lost my breast to cancer I did not want to loose my crown and glory as well so he told me that I would seeing a different doctor regarding my chemotherapy so a few days later I was back to the hospital having a talk with my oncologist he explained to me what was going to happen I then asked him if I would loose my hair he said no I would not loose my hair so there I was again given a date to attend my first chemotherapy session .

My first chemotherapy started on the 13th February 2001 as I sat in a chair Gordon sat in the other one and as the nurse was giving me my chemo in my right arm Gordon sat and took his watch to bits and he did not say anything to me he just sat there as if nothing was happening to me the receiving of the chemo was not as bad as I thought it would be and when they had finished with me they handed me a bag I asked what was in the bag they told me steroids and that I had to take them as I walked out of that hospital holding my bag of steroids I felt so weird in the head it was as if I was as high as a kite my first night I could not sleep I was wide awake most of the night I felt fine apart from the lack of sleep but as the week progressed I felt so ill I just wanted to die there and then my ankles swelled up as did my left arm and my fingers and on top this I felt so sick I could not eat any thing on the second week after my first chemo I lay in my bed and prayed for gods to help me get through this as I could not even get out of my bed I was so ill plus my hair was coming out I just lay in that bed and cried I could not even drink I was so tired but I could not sleep I was told it was because of the steroids but on the third week I felt a bit better then I was away back to square one as I had to have my chemo every three weeks I was in total agony my stomach was so sore I could not get the toilet I told Gordon that they should of let me die as I felt really ill with each chemo I received .

I was just about to receive my forth chemo when I told my oncologist that I wanted to stop my treatments as I could not take any more she told me I was doing fine as I only had another three sessions to go by this time I was ready to give up I told her no more she then asked me if I had any help from the Macmillan nurses regarding counselling I told her I never saw a Macmillan nurse since I came out of the hospital after the removal of my breast she told me that she would get a Macmillan nurse to come out to me then she asked me if I would take my chemotherapy I said yes even though I didn't want to so once again I sat there and received the chemotherapy through my right arm and the next day after my forth treatment I opened up my front door to a Macmillan nurse she told me once we got talking that she was sorry but I slipped through the net so it was just as well I was a strong person that got me through the last three chemo sessions so with the help from my friend Colleen and the Macmillan nurse I finished my last chemotherapy on the 13thJuly 2001 I was so glad it was all over and that I survived the worst.

A week later saw me back to my oncologist he then told me that I had to receive radiotherapy I asked him why he then told me it was just to make sure all the cancer was gone I asked him for a break he said that would be fine also I was asked if I was willing to do a trial for the radiotherapy I said yes to this as I told him if I can help others in the same situation then that was fine by me so the day of my first radiotherapy I was shown into this room just looking at that machine gave me palpitations and as I lay on the table I prayed for god to help me and as soon as I said this I felt a peace which I never felt before I felt so relaxed I could of slept on that table it was as if some one had put a nice warm blanket around my whole body I lay like this through the whole of my session I had to have radiotherapy in three different places on my body two at my breast area and one at my neck I had a whole week of radiotherapy and after my treatments I was told I would be seen in six months time at the oncologist clinic I had come through cancer and I was alive and kicking because if it were not for the fact my grandson nipped me I would have been dead as I was told after my second biopsy that I had the cancer for six months and I was told if I did not go to the hospital when I did then I would never of made it to the following year so as far as I was concerned it was a miracle.

SAMUEL

After I got over the cancer my son Samuel came into my mind a lot over the next few months I tried not to think about him as it was to painful for me to remember I tried to put these thoughts away back into my mind but the more I tried to do this the more they surfaced as some one or something was trying to tell me that the time had come to face up to the fact that I had a son and I had to go and find out what happened to him all those years ago so my first port of call was the social work department I phoned them up and asked what it is I have to do regards to some information about my son they told me to write a letter to the head of child services so I sat down that same day and I wrote a letter requesting some information about my son that was one letter I found very hard to do as I was writing it I was crying at the same time I had all these emotions going on inside of me all I saw in my mind was that day I went and took him out of the school in 1982 and how the social worker came and took him back and how I had to stand and watch as they took his little hand and led him out of my life for good as they told me I had lost all rights to him as his mum .

I posted the letter the same day and that night I sat up most of the night looking on adoption sites hoping that my son had posted on one of them I looked at dozens of these sights with regards to a male and with Samuels date of birth and who was from Scotland I joined birth mothers sites hoping against hope that some one would know all about Samuel every night and day I would spend hours on end looking for my son on these sites all I did was cry as I was looking at all these different posts from various adoptee some times I could not see the writing because of the tears that were in my eyes most nights I would go to bed with red swollen eyes the pain was to much I was hurting and crying inside I had to find my son to let him know I loved him very much and tell him the truth of what happened all those years ago .

It was about a week later I received a letter from the social work department telling me they found the records regarding my sons adoption and that I had to phone for an appointment to see a counsellor a Margery Fisher I asked my friend Colleen to go with me as something told me that I would need a witness to every thing that was said between this Margery Fisher and myself .

On the day of the appointment we were shown into this little room by Margery Fisher I was feeling very apprehensive as I knew that I had to go back in time to find out what happened as regard to my sons adoption so the first question I asked this Margery Fisher what exactly did happen to Samuel she told me that he was adopted in 1984 and that he had went to a couple who were school teachers and that they could no have kids of there own and that he was very lucky to be adopted by such a nice couple my heart was breaking as she told me all this then she told me that I did not want my son then I would change my mind and tell them I did want him I told her at that time of my life I was so confused and ill and I could not remember ever saying that or ever signing any adoption papers and if I did sign anything then I wanted to see the proof with my signature on it she went out of the room and she came back a few minutes later and told me that she could not find them I told her they must be in the file somewhere she then changed her story and told me that Gordon had signed over my son to them as I was so ill to make any decisions I told her that she was sitting there telling me lies as Gordon was not Samuels birth father and that he did not have the right to sign anything relating to Samuel then I asked her where was my son for two years as I was led to believe I had not right over my son in 1982 when social service took him out of my house after I had taken him out of the school she then told me that he was in a foster home as they could not adopted Samuel out until they had applied to the courts after two years to take my parental rights away I was so bloody angry when I heard her say this I told her away back in 1982 I had my rights all the time but because I was so ill they led me to believe I had lost all my parental rights at that time and as for Samuel going to this couple who could not have children of there own I told her that they stole my son from me as far as I am concerned that's exactly what they did do she then told me that I did not want my son any way again I argued with her and told her I was ill and that I was not going to sit there and feel guilty because of my illness then she had the nerve to tell me that as far as she was concerned I still needed help I refused to let this woman goat me into doing something that I would later regret so with gritted teeth I told her that as I was so ill as she put it they must of thought I would be dead a buried long before now and that they never thought for one minute that I was going to come back after twenty five years and make enquires about my son .

I then asked her if I had signed my sons adoption papers all those years ago then why did they have to put my son in care for two years she never answered this one she kept tripping herself up she could not give me any straight answers then she told me that Samuel was staying with this family away back in the 1982 and that something bad had happened and they had to take my son out of that house I was totally shocked when I heard this I asked her what it was that happened to my son she would not say by this time I was seething with rage and pain the thought of something happening to my son in a strangers house I was going crazy inside I then asked her if my son was abused in any way she said no and again I asked her what was so terrible that they had to take a five year old out of a home that they found for him she still would not answer me I felt like getting up and hitting this smug heartless bitch as that was all she was to me she sat there and she tried her best at making me feel a bad mother and I got the impression she wanted me to leave the past alone well I did not give a dam about what she thought I had a few sessions with this bitch and I never got any straight answers from her and each time I saw her my friend Colleen was with me and she even asked Colleen if she was in my life away back in 1982 and my friend said she was and that I never ever mentioned any thing about putting my son up for adoption so I have left all my details and Samuels with a adoption agency hoping and praying that my son does try to find me one day as he is my son and I am his mother and no one who ever they are will ever take that from me.

One day I received a phone call from my big brother he told me that my mother had died apparently she died during the night on the 5th April 2004 after I put the phone down I just cried and I was angry that she left this earth without telling anyone the truth of what happened to me all those years ago I was left with it all again she was out of the misery but I was right back into it again I was that bad I had to go back to counselling once more the nightmares came back to haunt me again plus my brother phoned and told me that the family did not want me at the funeral and that they had just been at my mothers house and emptied it of all things that was of value I asked about my mothers jewellery he told me it had all gone and that the reason they did this was to make sure I would not get any thing and apparently my mother had money in the bank and that apart from David my big brother the rest of my brothers did not want me to get my share I told David I was having my share as my mother owed me big time and that I wanted my place in the family as I was still there sister whether they liked it or not David agreed with me and he told me he managed to get me a ring and a few odd and ends this I accepted gladly as once again I went through the hurt period of losing my mother just like my father and I accepted it also I did not got to the funeral but I did go to the grave side and said my farewells to her there and I asked her why she did not tell every one the truth I just turned and walk away and that night I was staying with my daughter when I got up to go to the toilet and when I looked up I saw this light it shone bright then faded I knew it was my mother and I told her that I saw her and I told her that I had forgiven her and that she must go into the light.

A week after they buried my mother my brother David phoned me and told me that Mark had been diagnosed with stomach cancer and that it was inoperable I told him I was so sorry to hear this he then kept me informed of Marks illness and how it was progressing and a few months later I received a phone call from my brother David all the way from the Canada telling me that my brother Mark had died it was the 11th August 2004 this really upset me more than my parents as my brother died hating me and that was very hard for me to come to terms with and what made things worse for me was the fact I could not go to his funeral and that when they put his obituary in the paper my name was never mentioned it was as if I never existed and that broke my heart I was hurting inside because I had just lost my younger brother to cancer they all treat me with contempt apart from David and his family and there is only two people who caused all this bad blood and this was this my mother and father but mostly my mother but I cannot let it rule my life I forgave my mother and I must let the past stay in the past but some times it does come back with a vengeance especially when you are faced with hostility from your own brothers and nieces and cousins because every time my sisters oldest daughter sees me in the street or shops she gives me nothing but verbal abuse just because I told the truth about my father her grandfather as I have took the abuse for years I have learnt to live with it and I gather strength from it because every time my family throw abuse at me the more I fight back as I will let nothing or no one try to destroy me ever again as I know god saved me for a reason and that reason was to write this book to let others know they are not alone and that there is help out there and to never give up on life as they are special as god gave them life and that in itself is a miracle .

As for my younger brothers I feel sorry for them all as they are the ones carrying the bad feelings inside of them not me I don't hate them any more in fact every night I asked god to send his angles to them and to protect them as he has protected me all my life as I know it was my mother who poisoned there minds against me and they grew up with these bad thoughts of me she did a good job turning my own family against me and I know they will never accept me as there sister as I have been fazed out of the family for to long now also I accept that it must be hard for them to believe me when I spoke about the sexual abuse from my father and that they don't want to face up to the fact that there father was a paedophile as that was exactly what he was.